PICKWICK PAPERS

NOTES

including
- *Critical Biography*
- *Introduction*
- *List of Characters*
- *Synopsis*
- *Summaries and Commentaries*
- *Critical Commentary*
- *Review Questions*
- *Selected Bibliography*

by
James Weigel, Jr.

D0814874

INCORPORATED

LINCOLN, NEBRASKA 68501

Editor

Gary Carey, M.A.
University of Colorado

Consulting Editor

James L. Roberts, Ph.D.
Department of English
University of Nebraska

Cliffs Notes, Inc.   Lincoln, Nebraska

CONTENTS

Pickwick Papers Notes

CRITICAL BIOGRAPHY

The attention that has been paid to the life of Charles Dickens is due mainly to his stature as the greatest novelist of Victorian England. Even though the biographical accounts of Dickens frequently try to unravel the mystery of his creative genius, there is something about Dickens' imaginative power that defies explanation in purely biographical terms. Nevertheless, his biography shows the source of that power and is the best place to begin to define it.

The second child of John and Elizabeth Dickens, Charles was born on February 7, 1812, in Portsea on England's south coast. At that time John Dickens was stationed in Portsmouth as a clerk in the Navy Pay Office. The family was of lower-middle-class origins, John having come from servants and Elizabeth from minor bureaucrats. Dickens' father was vivacious and generous but had an unfortunate tendency to live beyond his means. His mother was affectionate and rather inept in practical matters. Dickens would later use his father as the basis for Mr. Micawber and would portray his mother as Mrs. Nickleby—two marvelous comic figures.

After a transfer to London in 1814 the family moved to Chatham, near Rochester, three years later. Dickens was about five at the time, and for the next five years his life was pleasant. Taught to read by his mother, he devoured his father's small collection of classics, which included Shakespeare, Cervantes, Defoe, Smollett, Fielding, and Goldsmith. These left a permanent mark on his imagination. He also went to some performances of Shakespeare, and these helped to influence his lifelong attraction to the theater. Dickens attended school during this period and showed himself to be a rather solitary, observant, good-natured child with some talent for comic routines, which his father encouraged. In retrospect Dickens looked upon these years as a kind of golden age. His first novel, *Pickwick Papers,* is in part an attempt to recapture their idyllic nature; it exalts innocence and the youthful spirit, and its happiest scenes take place in that geographical area.

In the light of the family's move back to London, where financial calamity overtook the Dickenses, the time in Chatham must have seemed glorious indeed. The family moved into the shabby suburb of Camden Town, and Dickens was taken out of school and set to menial jobs about the household. In time, to help augment the family income, Dickens was given a job in a blacking factory among coarse companions. Then his father was jailed for debt in Marshalsea Prison for three months. Dickens worked at washing and labeling blacking bottles for six months or so. Years later he reported to his closest friend, John Forster, that he felt a deep sense of abandonment, of being forsaken, at this time. His feelings of lostness and humiliation emphasize the fact that the major themes of his art may be traced to this period. His sympathy for the poor and the victimized, his fascination with prisons and money, his desire to vindicate his heroes' status as gentlemen, and the notion of London as an awesome and rather threatening environment all appear to have their roots in these experiences, which resulted from the brief but nearly total collapse of his parents' ability to protect him from the world. Out on his own at an early age, Dickens acquired a lasting self-reliance, driving ambition, and a boundless energy that went into everything he did. In many ways Dickens never outgrew the shocks and emotional attitudes of this period, but his achievement is that he worked these shocks over in novel after novel until they took on the symbolic complexity and depth of great literature.

At thirteen Dickens went back to school for two years and then took a job in a lawyer's office. Dissatisfied with the work, he learned shorthand and became a freelance court reporter in 1828. The work was seasonal and enabled him to do a good deal of reading in the British Museum. At the age of twenty Dickens became a full-fledged journalist, working for three papers in succession. In the next four to five years he acquired the reputation of being the fastest and most accurate parliamentary reporter in London. The value of these years was that he gained a sound, firsthand knowledge of London and the provinces which helped him flesh out the experiences of early adolescence with concrete details and a maturer experience of the world.

In December, 1833, Dickens began to publish sketches of London and its inhabitants in the *Monthly Magazine*. In time he began to sign them with the pseudonym, "Boz," and gained some notice for the dramatic quality of his reportage. On his twenty-fourth birthday these articles were published in book form as *Sketches by Boz, Illustrative of Everyday Life and Everyday People*. Although the book was a success it had little intrinsic literary merit. However, it launched him on his career as a writer, a career astonishing in its productivity, quality, and undiminished popular acclaim.

A week after his first book was published the firm of Chapman and Hall approached Dickens about writing a series of fillers to accompany sporting illustrations by a well-known artist. Dickens convinced the firm that the illustrations should follow the text, rather than vice versa, and began writing the first installment of *The Posthumous Papers of the Pickwick Club,* which appeared in April, 1836. Writing in monthly installments was a mode of publication that proved congenial to Dickens. In the beginning it enabled him to continue his newspaper work and later to edit magazines. Writing for deadlines inflicted a lack of artistic coherence on his early novels, but eventually he was able to abandon his episodic structures and impose a tighter, more unified organization on his later novels.

The *Pickwick Papers* got off to a slow start, but with the introduction of Sam Weller its sales skyrocketed into the tens of thousands. A Pickwick rage started and Dickens' success was assured. On the surface this novel is a series of sketches, loosely held together by the adventures of Samuel Pickwick and his friends. Yet there are certain basic themes that unify the novel: the celebration of travel, benevolence, youthfulness, fellowship, plenty, romance; the contrast between the freedom of the open road and the constriction of Fleet Prison; the comic treatment of various institutions and professions; and the gradual revelation of Mr. Pickwick's endearing humanity.

With the prospect of a livable income Dickens, at twenty-four, married Catherine Hogarth, the daughter of a newspaper colleague. The marriage was genuinely happy at first and there were ten children. Catherine seems to have been a gentle, loving woman, but rather commonplace and lethargic, without much aptitude for housekeeping or child-rearing. Under the strain of personality conflicts, the steady pressure of Dickens' numerous activities, and his infatuation with Ellen Ternan, the couple separated twenty-two years later in disagreeable circumstances.

Dickens' domestic life, in fact, was odd from the start. The man who sentimentalized marriage was prone to falling in love with other women, including his sisters-in-law. The relationship with Ellan Ternan may have begun platonically, but the evidence points to the fact that she eventually became his mistress. Moreover, his treatment of his own children was harsh, even as he made his readers weep over the fates of innocent and victimized fictional children. This does not mean that Dickens was an out-and-out hypocrite. In his novels he projected what most men want at home — an affectionate, tidy, understanding, attentive

8

wife. And he really knew what it meant to be a lost child in an incomprehensible world. But like many hyperactive public men, Dickens was spoiled and impatient. He craved attention, and between his demands and those of his children the marriage fell to pieces. His writing was partly an attempt to redress his unsatisfactory personal life, and in doing so it appealed to many with similar discontents.

While still working on his *Pickwick Papers* (1836-37), Dickens contracted to write two more novels and started publishing *Oliver Twist* (1837-38). During this period he also worked on a second series of *Sketches by Boz* (1839). *Oliver Twist* marked a new departure for Dickens, presenting an attack on workhouse conditions and London's criminal-infested slums through the nightmarish experiences of an innocent young boy. Oliver's trials are rewarded in the end when his claim to gentility is established once and for all. Before he had completed that novel Dickens began *Nicholas Nickleby* (1838-39), an exposure of private schools for unwanted boys. The hero this time actively seeks a gentlemanly position in life, whereas Oliver is a passive character. The private school, the slums, the workhouse are degrading conditions, analogous in some respects to prison. The only proper alternative is gentility. Dickens was extremely concerned with status, and in these two novels the drama centers upon those who try to deprive the hero of status and those who try to abet him. Each of these novels was successful and increased Dickens' readership. Unquestionably Dickens had hit upon a theme which interested a large proportion of the English middle class.

The next novel, *The Old Curiosity Shop* (1840-41), increased Dickens' popularity still further and stunned the public with the sentimental death of Little Nell. The heroine's urge to leave the corrupt, threatening city and find a pastoral peace and security may represent a drive toward death. London, for all its sinister aspects, is the center of vitality in the novel, while the countryside is rich in graveyards and moldering churches.

Even at this early stage in his career Dickens was capable of ambiguous feelings about the central subjects of his novels. He wrote about things that made him uneasy, that raised serious questions in his mind. His novels, in effect, were attempts to answer those questions about the city, prison, crime, success, and gentility. Time and again he came back to these subjects because his questions were of a kind that can never be answered conclusively. By reworking the old themes his art gained in subtlety, resonance, and depth. To the end of his career he never stopped growing.

Barnaby Rudge (1841) centered on London's anti-Catholic riots of 1780 and examined the relationship between vicious or misguided fathers and the obtuse, selfish authority of public institutions. Just as youth must rebel against the former, so society at large rebels against the latter; but in rebelling everyone is harmed. A historical novel, *Barnaby Rudge* shows that Dickens had learned much from Sir Walter Scott.

In 1842 Dickens and his wife took a trip to America, which resulted in an unflattering travel book, *American Notes* (1842), and in *Martin Chuzzlewit* (1843-44); this novel is flawed in structure, yet it explores various kinds of egoism with extraordinary verve. In a world where egoism predominates, we get an anarchic view of society. Even the hero is infected with selfishness and his success in establishing himself in the world is very precarious. In America he meets egoism in its most predatory form and returns to England chastened and poverty-stricken. He may win at last through his grandfather's generosity but he clearly exists in a world where strife is ever ready to devour him. Despite the grim sound of these comments, the novel is actually a comic *tour de force*.

Dombey and Son (1846-48) also has a flawed hero in Mr. Dombey. The fault is inhuman pride of position, which undergoes three crises: the death of a son, the desertion by a proud wife, and the collapse of a financial empire. Dickens uses this subject to show the changing Victorian world, and he balances Dombey's pride and the forces of change with the unchanging love of Dombey's daughter, Florence. *Dombey and Son* marks Dickens' first major attempt to portray English society realistically. This novel is technically superior to his earlier works, but the comic inventiveness is not nearly as flamboyant. As Dickens' organizing skill grew in his succeeding novels, the comic flair diminished, transforming itself into satire.

For his eighth novel, *David Copperfield* (1849-50), he made use of autobiographical material. Copperfield's early hardship and rise to prominence is a thinly disguised version of Dickens' own life. This was Dickens' first effort to show the education of a hero from the inside, using a first-person narration. The interest of the book lies in the peripheral characters and intrigues as the raw material of Copperfield's growth.

The most remarkable thing about Dickens is that from his first novel to his last he never ceased to experiment with his forms, themes, and characters. Each novel built on the previous ones and yet was an effort at something new and fresh. With *Bleak House* (1852-53), for example, he used Chancery and its legal obfuscations to serve as a metaphor for society at large and to connect every class from the aristocratic Dedlocks to Jo the street-sweeper. Moreover, he set the omniscient third-person narrative side by side with a first-person narrative to get a dual vision of the Victorian mental climate. This kind of experimentation enhanced his popularity, yet it was an important element in his greatness as well.

In *Hard Times* (1854) Dickens combined the moral fable with a realistic social analysis in his depiction of an industrial town. The school and the factory are the confining, objective equivalents of the narrow views of the English political economists. As an alternative to the grim social environment Dickens shows the freedom and good-heartedness of a circus troupe. As Dickens grew older benevolence has a harder time of it in his novels. It is no longer dished out wholesale by pleasant gentlemen of unlimited means. More and more it becomes personal, intimate, the expression of love in an increasingly hostile environment.

Dickens' next novel, *Little Dorrit* (1855-57), presents no alternative to the vision of society as a series of interrelated prisons. From top to bottom all the world's a jail, and no one can escape it. The best that can be salvaged from this claustrophobic society is the mild, tender affection between Arthur Clennam and Amy Dorrit, both of whom are overshadowed by Marshalsea Prison.

However, in *A Tale of Two Cities* (1859) Dickens finds an uneasy solution to the prison-like nature of the Victorian world. As society dissolves into anarchy, the only redeeming values are friendship, family, heroic self-sacrifice — each of which is based on love. As a solution to the nightmare of history these values are far more satisfactory than those embodied in the circus troupe of *Hard Times* because they are deeper and more universal.

Prison also plays a role in *Great Expectations* (1860-61). Using a first-person narrator-hero, as in *David Copperfield*, Dickens shows how money and status corrupt people. Crime and prison represent the most dramatic form of that corruption, the dark side of Pip's gentility. Here Dickens returned to his early theme of the young man trying to make good as a gentleman. But this time the theme is shot through with irony because Pip's rise in society is based on a convict's money. In this novel Dickens places redemption in good, honest work.

Our Mutual Friend (1864-65) is Dickens' last completed novel. Through an omniscient narrator Dickens explores the corrupting taint of money in the whole of society. Here he stresses the regenerating force of love rather than that of work. This novel combines a large, vivid cast of characters with great structural proficiency, and may well be Dickens' best novel.

His last work, *The Mystery of Edwin Drood* (1870), remained unfinished. It turns away from society and concentrates on private pathology, on the double nature of John Jasper, a murderer. It is almost Dostoievskian in its view of the criminal as a tormented man fallen from grace and yet having a very respectable facade. It was characteristic of Dickens that the work on which he was working at the time of his death should mark still another new departure. *Edwin Drood* is a tantalizing piece of work.

Dickens' body of novels remains his outstanding achievement, a living testament to his intensely creative life. But he wrote much else besides: volumes of excellent journalistic essays, two travel books, several hundred letters, a book of Christmas stories, a child's history of England. He also edited three magazines, two of these for many years.

Furthermore, Dickens was very much involved in theater work during the whole of his career. He frequented the theater and, for a time, considered becoming a professional actor. He wrote plays, acted in amateur productions (which were really quite skilled), and he directed plays with an impressive energy and thoroughness. In time his theatrical bent found an outlet in his public readings from his novels. These readings overwhelmed audiences, yet the strain of doing them hastened his death.

Dickens practiced benevolence as well as preached it. In his private life he did many favors for his parents, his brothers and sisters, and his in-laws, the Hogarths. In public he organized charities and gave benefits, contributing substantial amounts. In this capacity he worked with the heiress, Angela Burdett-Coutts, for many years.

Physically, Dickens had a slight and rather frail body, but he was very active. He loved taking twenty-mile walks, horseback riding, making journeys, entertaining friends, dining well, and playing practical jokes. He enjoyed games of charades with his family, was an expert amateur magician, and practiced hypnotism. One tends to share Shaw's opinion that Dickens was always on stage. He was the quintessence of a master of ceremonies: ebullient, dynamic, quick, observant, full of zest for life. Yet he was also high-strung, impatient, irascible, and subject to fits of depression. At times he must have been nearly intolerable to live with, however agreeable he may have been as a companion.

In view of his strenuous life it was not surprising that he died, prematurely aged, of a stroke at fifty-eight. At his death on June 9, 1870, he was immensely popular, wealthy, and probably the greatest writer the Victorian age produced. Perhaps his broadest achievement lay in the part his towering novels played in raising the novel from a slightly disreputable level to the dominant form it is today.

Appropriately, Dickens was buried in the Poets' Corner of Westminster Abbey and was mourned internationally.

INTRODUCTION TO *PICKWICK PAPERS*

Pickwick Papers is one of the most popular novels of all time. Since its first publication in serial form in 1836 it has enjoyed an immense success. It inspired Pickwick products, literary imitations and plagiarisms, and state adaptations. Most "smash hits" are quickly forgotten, but this novel is still read for enjoyment by general readers. Moreover, in England today there are men who retrace the imaginary travels of the Pickwickians, as if to recreate the world of the novel. The reasons for its universal popularity are not hard to find. The novel is funny, easy to read, rich in characterization, humane and Christian in its values, lively and continuously entertaining — in short, a thorough delight. *Pickwick Papers* is a publisher's dream: the perennial best-seller.

This is essentially a serious novel, but its serious aspects are presented in the guise of comedy. Not that Dickens makes the reader swallow a bitter pill with a sugar coating of humor. The important values are precisely those that blend well with comedy. *Pickwick Papers* exalts the joys of travel, the pleasures of eating and drinking well, fellowship between men, innocence, benevolence, youthfulness and romance. Dickens achieves these values by presenting them against rather unpleasant realities. Comfortable travel is contrasted with the stagnant squalor of Fleet Prison. Good food and drink are played off against the grubby victuals and wine of prison. Male friendships are set off against predatory wives, widows, and spinsters as well as mean and unscrupulous men. Innocence and youthfulness are subjected to skepticism,

knavery, and prison. And romance is contrasted with various schemes
for mercenary marriages. As a result we get a full picture of just how
valuable these qualities and conditions are. Through contrasts
the reader comes to cherish goodness and simplicity as they are embodied in Mr. Pickwick. But, again, we experience them through the
medium of comedy.

Perhaps the most noticeable feature of the novel is its masculine
quality. It isn't simply that the great majority of the characters are male
or that most of the women are treated unsympathetically. And certainly
the major characters are not particularly aggressive, violent, or domi-
neering. The masculinity of the novel rests mainly in the finesse and
accuracy of Dickens' portrayal of male relationships. Women are shown
either as sweet young objects of romance or as threatening middle-aged
predators. They are either sentimental or comic figures and lack the
reality with which Dickens draws men. Dickens understands men and
delights in their eccentricities, but women are an unknown quantity
to him. If a woman wants some idea of the world most men live in she
could do no better than to read this novel.

Dickens did go on to write greater, subtler, more complex novels,
but *Pickwick Papers* can be viewed as a testing ground for themes and
characters in his later works, even if the plot is loose and rambling,
closer in form to the picaresque novels of the eighteenth century than
to Dickens' later novels or to the future development of the novel. The
themes of money, incarceration, and fatherhood are treated extensively,
but Dickens would take them up later and develop them to a high de-
gree of virtuosity.

Dickens did not come to *Pickwick Papers* without literary
precedents, fresh as it seems in the history of the novel. Behind the
episodic form lay the work of Cervantes, Fielding, and Smollett. Behind the idea of the Pickwick Club and its leader lay the adventures of
Surtees' Jorrocks. Behind the treatment of the law lay Fielding's depiction of legal corruption. The farcical scenes of men getting caught in
nightclothes have their counterparts in Fielding and Smollett. The idea
of a man going to prison on principle and changing into a wiser, better
man was already used by Goldsmith in *The Vicar of Wakefield*. And in
back of the treatment of various scenes lay a broad acquaintance with
the theater and its techniques. In the case of Smollett, Fielding, and
Surtees, Dickens changed their coarseness and brutality into a gentler
kind of comedy. And he secularized the otherworldliness of Goldsmith's
vicar. Although the sources are present, they are not obtrusive. And

Pickwick Papers addresses itself to the reader as an original work — original in the sense that one finds a new prospect opening in the development of the novel and a fresh prose style to express it.

From a sociological standpoint, however, the novel has a serious deficiency. If politics and elections are treated scornfully as a species of nonsense that is useless for effecting good, how is the evil of a debtors' prison to be eliminated? By implication Dickens places hope of society's redemption in the private hands of philanthropists like Mr. Pickwick, rather than in institutions. But personal benevolence is totally impotent against bad institutions: Mr. Pickwick can do little to alleviate the misery of the Fleet. Dickens obviously feels that debtors' prisons should be done away with, but he burnt his bridges behind him in showing political action to be futile.

But Dickens was not a sociologist or a political economist. As a novelist he was much more effective in calling attention to social problems — like debtors' prisons — than he would have been in proposing solutions. He had the power to make his readers visualize Fleet Prison, which was much more effective in the cause of reform than any number of tracts. A novelist can muster the tides of public opinion, which Dickens knew better than any of his critics. He can arrange his fiction so that it produces indignation. Dickens was a reformer not by virtue of his intellectual ability but by virtue of the spell he cast over his readers, making them feel certain injustices as if they were their own.

If *Pickwick Papers* is a literary triumph, it is also something of a social triumph. Although there had been movements for reforming and abolishing debtors' prisons long before Dickens wrote this book, he helped give the movement the force of public opinion. He was assisted by a gentleman named Samuel Pickwick. Within about two decades debtors' prisons no longer existed in London.

LIST OF CHARACTERS

Samuel Pickwick

Founder of the Pickwick Club and hero of the novel, a fat, bald, elderly, innocent, generous, benevolent gentleman. His adventures and developing character are the center of interest.

Tracy Tupman

Fat and middle-aged, he fancies himself to be the romantic adventurer of the Pickwick Club. He has an unhappy flirtation with Rachael Wardle.

Augustus Snodgrass

A young, innocuous fellow, he poses as the poet of the Pickwick Club, although he never writes a line of verse. He falls in love with Emily Wardle and marries her.

Nathaniel Winkle

A very inept young sportsman, Winkle has a flair for misadventures. A member of the Pickwick Club, he enlists Mr. Pickwick's aid in his romance and marriage with Arabella Allen.

Mr. Blotton

An unpleasant member of the club with a keen eye for humbug.

Alfred Jingle

A romantic adventurer who schemes for various mercenary marriages, which Mr. Pickwick tries to thwart. He is brought low in the Fleet Prison and rehabilitated by Mr. Pickwick.

Dr. Slammer

An army man who challenges Winkle to a duel at Rochester, he is irascible and has a taste for violence when frustrated.

Lieutenant Tappleton

Dr. Slammer's second at the duel, a stickler for rules.

Dr. Payne

A savage army man who attends the duel to see bloodshed.

Jem Hutley (Dismal Jemmy)

A cadaverous strolling actor who tells the Pickwickians a morbid tale.

Colonel and Mrs. Bulder

Members of Rochester society.

Sir Thomas Clubber

Another member of Rochester society.

Mr. Wardle

A hospitable country squire at Dingley Dell. Fond of the Pickwickians, he entertains them on several occasions.

Emily Wardle

Mr. Wardle's pert, pretty daughter, Snodgrass' sweetheart.

Isabella Wardle

Mr. Wardle's other pretty daughter, who marries Mr. Trundle during the Christmas festivities.

Rachael Wardle

Mr. Wardle's spinster sister, she flirts with Tupman and unsuccessfully elopes with Jingle.

Mrs. Wardle

Mr. Wardle's partly deaf, cantankerous old mother.

Joe the Fat Boy

A gluttonous, sleepy servant to Mr. Wardle.

Mr. Trundle

Isabella Wardle's colorless fiancé and husband.

An old clergyman

A storyteller with a cheerful disposition and a gloomy mind at Wardles'.

Mr. Miller

A neighbor of Wardles' who puts his foot in his mouth.

Sam Weller

A shrewd, cocky, clever, affectionate cockney boot cleaner and general handyman whom Mr. Pickwick engages as a servant, and who becomes Mr. Pickwick's closest friend.

Mr. Perker

A brisk little attorney for Mr. Wardle and Mr. Pickwick. He admires legal chicanery but has a good heart and is a friend to his two clients.

Mrs. Martha Bardell

Mr. Pickwick's landlady, she assumes he has proposed to her and sues for breach of promise. Thrown in jail because she cannot pay her legal fees, Mr. Pickwick has her released.

Master Tommy Bardell

Her squalling young son.

Mr. Pott

Editor of the *Eatanswill Gazette*, a pompous, vindictive, cowardly, henpecked man.

Mrs. Pott

His aggressive wife, who becomes fond of Winkle, throws hysterics, and eventually leaves her husband.

Mr. Slurk

Editor of the *Eatanswill Independent*, Mr. Pott's enemy.

The Hon. Samuel Slumkey

The Blue candidate and winner of the Eatanswill election.

The Hon. Horatio Fizkin

The Buff candidate at the Eatanswill election.

The one-eyed bagman

A traveling salesman who tells stories at Eatanswill and Bristol.

Mrs. Leo Hunter

A fatuous celebrity-hunter at Eatanswill.

Mr. Leo Hunter

Her stiff, servile husband.

Count Smorltork

A silly foreigner at Mrs. Hunter's party.

Job Trotter

A cunning, emaciated actor whom Alfred Jingle employs as a servant.

Miss Tomkins

The headmistress of the boarding school at Bury St. Edmunds, where Mr. Pickwick is taken prisoner.

Captain Boldwig

A ferocious country squire near Bury St. Edmunds, he has the drunken Mr. Pickwick carted to the animal pound.

Peter Lowten

Mr. Perker's cynical law clerk.

Dodson and **Fogg**

The unscrupulous law partners who handle Mrs. Bardell's lawsuit.

Mr. Jackson

Dodson and Fogg's oily law clerk.

Jack Bamber

A half-crazed, seedy law clerk, he relates a wild tale.

Peter Magnus

A nervous, jealous suitor who involves the Pickwickians in trouble at Ipswich.

Miss Witherfield

His hysterical middle-aged fiancée.

George Nupkins, Esq.

The windbag magistrate at Ipswich, an ignorant, henpecked man.

Mrs. Nupkins

His nasty, social-climbing wife.

Miss Henrietta Nupkins

Their nasty daughter, she has a crush on Jingle.

Daniel Grummer

An officious police captain who arrests the Pickwickians in Ipswich.

Mr. Dubbley

A big policeman in Ipswich.

Mr. Jinks

The timid court clerk in Ipswich.

Mr. Muzzle

Nupkins' butler.

Tony Weller

Sam Weller's fat, kindly, irresponsible father, a coachman plagued by domestic trouble.

Susan Weller

Tony Weller's self-righteously pious, hypocritical wife, who has taken up with a disreputable preacher.

The Reverend Stiggins

An avaricious, alcoholic, unsavory evangelist who sponges off the Wellers.

Anthony Humm

A temperance lecturer at a meeting Sam and Tony Weller attend.

Mrs. Betsy Cluppins

A nosy, piggish friend of Mrs. Bardell's.

Mrs. Susannah Sanders

Another friend of Mrs. Bardell's.

Arabella Allen

Winkle's pert, attractive sweetheart and wife.

Ben Allen

Her doltish brother, who wants her to marry Bob Sawyer.

Bob Sawyer

A medical student and prankster who wants to marry Arabella.

Jack Hopkins

A medical student who is full of curious, funny anecdotes.

Mrs. Mary Ann Raddle

Bob Sawyer's vituperative landlady and a friend of Mrs. Bardell's.

Mr. Raddle

Her ineffectual, inarticulate husband.

Serjeant Snubbin

Mr. Pickwick's untidy, abstracted, ineffective court lawyer.

Mr. Mallard

His spruce, impressive secretary.

Mr. Phunky

Serjeant Snubbin's nervous assistant at the trial.

Serjeant Buzfuz

Mrs. Bardell's prosecuting attorney, an orotund, silly, but effective lawyer.

Mr. Justice Stareleigh

The fat, nasty, inattentive judge at Mr. Pickwick's trial.

Colonel Dowler

A vociferous, cowardly, jealous man who challenges Winkle to a duel at Bath and then retreats.

Mrs. Dowler

His hapless, partying wife.

Mrs. Craddock

Mr. Pickwick's landlady at Bath.

Angelo Cyrus Bantam, Esq.

The master of ceremonies at Bath, a dapper, ignorant, gregarious man.

John Smauker

His snooty footman, who invites Sam Weller to a "swarry."

Mrs. Wugsby

A fashionable, rather nasty woman at Bath.

Lady Snuphanuph

Another fashionable woman at Bath.

Mary

Sam Weller's sweetheart. Originally the Nupkins' housemaid, she helps Sam find Arabella Allen at Bristol, assists in Winkle's elopement, and becomes the Winkle housemaid.

A scientific gentleman

An old man whose desire for fame leads him to mistake Mr. Pickwick's lantern light for a "scientific" phenomenon.

Mr. Tom Roker

The warder and supply man at Fleet Prison, he charges high rates for meager lodgings and furniture.

Neddy

His indolent companion.

The Chancery prisoner

The pathetic, dying man from whom Mr. Pickwick rents his prison cell.

23

Mr. Smangle

The shifty, predatory prisoner with whom Mr. Pickwick spends his first night.

Mr. Mivins (The Zephyr)

Smangle's obnoxious, clowning companion.

Mr. Solomon Pell

The seedy, self-advertising lawyer in the debtors' court. The Wellers become his clients.

Arabella Allen's aunt

The guardian of Arabella, she is horrified when her niece elopes.

Mr. Martin

The aunt's taciturn servant, who is attacked by Ben Allen.

Mr. Winkle, Sr.

A hard-headed businessman, he is suspicious of his son's marriage until he meets Arabella.

Wilkins Flasher, Esq.

A dapper stockbroker who bets on every topic of conservation.

CHARACTERS FROM THE INTERPOLATED TALES

John

The alcoholic pantomimist of "The Stroller's Tale." He drinks himself to death and abuses his wife and son in the process.

John Edmunds

The convict in "The Convict's Return." He causes the death of his mother and father and dies repentant.

A Madman

Author of "The Madman's Manuscript." He finds his wife does not love him and takes a lunatic revenge on her and her brother.

Tom Smart

The cocky hero of "The Bagman's Tale," who saves a widow from a scoundrel.

Nathaniel Pipkin

A schoolmaster in "The Parish Clerk." He loses Maria Lobbs and her father's money to a handsome cousin of Maria's.

George Heyling

A prisoner in "The Strange Client." Upon his release he exacts a prolonged revenge on his father-in-law.

Gabriel Grub

The misanthropic sexton in "The Goblins Who Stole a Sexton." Goblins convert him to love of his fellow man.

Prince Bladud

The unhappy prince of "The True Legend of Prince Bladud." He rebels against his vicious father and finds misery.

Jack Martin

The bagman's hard-drinking uncle in "The Bagman's Uncle." He rescues a lady from two villains during a ghostly coach ride.

BRIEF SYNOPSIS

In May, 1827, the Pickwick Club of London, headed by Samuel Pickwick, decides to establish a traveling society in which four members journey about England and make reports on their travels. The four members are Mr. Pickwick, a kindly retired businessman and philosopher whose thoughts never rise above the commonplace; Tracy Tupman, a ladies' man who never makes a conquest; Augustus Snodgrass, a poet who never writes a poem; and Nathaniel Winkle, a sportsman of tremendous ineptitude.

The Pickwickians meet to begin their first journey and get knocked about by an angry cabman, who thinks they are informers, while an angry crowd gathers. They are rescued by Alfred Jingle, who travels with them to Rochester. Jingle is an adventurer interested in wealthy women, and on this first trip he involves the innocent Winkle in a duel with Dr. Slammer, a hot-tempered army man.

At Chatham the Pickwickians watch army maneuvers, get buffeted about, and meet Mr. Wardle, a country squire who invites them to his estate at Dingley Dell. After some mishaps with horses Mr. Pickwick and his friends arrive at Mr. Wardle's Manor Farm, where they enjoy card games, flirting, storytelling, hunting, and a cricket match. Mr. Tupman falls in love with Mr. Wardle's spinster sister, Rachael; and Mr. Snodgrass falls in love with his daughter, Emily. However, Tupman is outsmarted by the vivacious, unscrupulous Jingle, who elopes with Rachael. Mr. Pickwick and Mr. Wardle pursue Jingle and Rachael to London, where, with the help of a lawyer, Mr. Perker, they buy off Jingle and save Rachael Wardle from an unhappy marriage.

In London Mr. Pickwick comes across Sam Weller, a boot cleaner and general handyman whom he takes on as a valet. Sam is a cockney man of the world: witty, intelligent, handy with his fists. When Mr. Pickwick tells his widowed landlady, Mrs. Bardell, that he has taken on a servant, she assumes from the ambiguous way he puts it that he intends to marry her. Mrs. Bardell faints in his arms just as Tupman, Snodgrass, and Winkle enter—a compromising circumstance.

Sam Weller's father, Tony, a coachman who had the misfortune to marry a widow, provides a running commentary through the novel on the dangers of matrimony. Tony's wife has taken up with a hypocritical, alcoholic evangelist and makes life miserable for her husband until her death. Both Tony Weller and Mr. Pickwick are prey for widows, because Mrs. Bardell soon starts a breach-of-promise suit against Mr. Pickwick.

Meanwhile, Mr. Pickwick and his friends go to Eatanswill to witness an election, which is both violent and nonsensical. Mr. Pickwick and Winkle stay with Mr. Pott, the editor of a partisan newspaper, and

Winkle unwittingly becomes involved in Pott's domestic fights. During their visit to Eatanswill the Pickwickians are invited to a costume party given by the local literary lioness, Mrs. Leo Hunter, where several varieties of silliness are exhibited. At this party Mr. Pickwick sees Alfred Jingle, whom he pursues to a neighboring town. Jingle's servant tells Mr. Pickwick that Jingle has designs on a young lady at a boarding school, and Mr. Pickwick decides to prevent the elopement. However, this information is a ruse that leads to Mr. Pickwick's embarrassment and an attack of rheumatism. The Pickwickians assemble at Bury St. Edmunds, where Mr. Wardle is on a hunting trip, and Mr. Pickwick recovers enough to go along. There he learns that Mrs. Bardell has filed suit against him through Dodson and Fogg, a pair of rascally lawyers. So Mr. Pickwick returns to London to see about getting legal help.

In London Mr. Pickwick learns that Jingle is in Ipswich and goes there to expose him. Because of a mix-up in bedrooms at an Ipswich Inn Mr. Pickwick is hauled before the justice, a local henpecked tyrant called Mr. Nupkins. Nupkins is visited frequently by Jingle, who is interested in the daughter. Mr. Pickwick extricates himself by proving that Jingle is an adventurer.

Eventually the Pickwickians return to the Wardle farm to celebrate Christmas and the wedding of Mr. Wardle's daughter, Isabella. Amid festivities Snodgrass continues his romance with Emily, and Winkle falls in love with Arabella Allen, a friend of Mr. Wardle's daughters.

On Valentine's Day, 1831, Mr. Pickwick is tried for breach of promise. Due to the rhetorical allegations of Serjeant Buzfuz and to the circumstantial evidence, Mr. Pickwick is found guilty and ordered to pay damages, which he refuses to do.

Since it is two months before Dodson and Fogg can have him jailed, the Pickwickians make a trip to Bath. There Winkle gets into more difficulties over a middle-aged woman and flees to Bristol, where he learns that his sweetheart, Arabella Allen, has been hidden by her brother. Sam Weller and Mr. Pickwick arrive in Bristol, where they help Winkle find Arabella in order to declare his intentions.

On returning to London Mr. Pickwick is taken to the Fleet Prison for debtors because he will not pay damages. In prison he witnesses much misery, filth, and squalor and for a brief time he is victimized by two predatory inmates. There he finds Alfred Jingle and his servant in utter destitution and gives them some assistance. Mr. Pickwick tells

Sam Weller to leave him, but Sam has himself jailed for debt to be with his kindly master. Dismayed by the misery of prison, Mr. Pickwick rents a cell by himself and comes out only in the evenings. When Mrs. Bardell is arrested and jailed because she cannot pay her lawyers, Mr. Pickwick begins to soften. Further, Winkle has married Arabella and needs Mr. Pickwick to intercede for them with her brother and his own father. Finally Mr. Pickwick decides to pay costs, which releases himself and Mrs. Bardell, and he also pays Jingle's debts.

Mr. Pickwick goes to Bristol to tell Ben Allen about Arabella's marriage, and Ben adjusts to the fact with the help of much liquor. Mr. Pickwick then goes to Birmingham to tell Winkle's father, who appears angry and disgusted by the news.

Back in London Mr. Pickwick pays Dodson and Fogg, sends Jingle and his servant to the West Indies to begin afresh, and learns that Emily Wardle is planning to elope with Snodgrass. Mr. Pickwick convinces Mr. Wardle that Snodgrass is a worthy gentleman, and the couple are married in Mr. Pickwick's newly purchased home. In the meantime Sam Weller has been courting a pretty housemaid named Mary, and under Mr. Pickwick's auspices they are married. And, though the London Pickwick Club has been dissolved, Samuel Pickwick lives to be godfather to many children.

SUMMARIES AND COMMENTARIES

CHAPTER 1

Summary

On May 12, 1827, the Pickwick Club of London listens to Mr. Pickwick's paper, "Speculations on the Source of the Hampstead Ponds, with some Observations on the Theory of Tittlebats." In order to extend the field of Mr. Pickwick's knowledge the club votes for a traveling society that will consist of Samuel Pickwick, Tracy Tupman, Augustus Snodgrass, and Nathaniel Winkle. Each will have to pay his own expenses and send reports back to the club. A fat, elderly, bald man, Mr. Pickwick is facetiously presented as a profound thinker. Tupman is a fat, middle-aged ladies' man, Snodgrass is a poet, and Winkle is a sportsman.

The club chairman, Mr. Pickwick, climbs up on a chair to make a speech about his desire to benefit mankind through scientific knowledge and about the danger of accidents in travel, to which a member called Blotton objects, telling him he is a humbug. Mr. Pickwick is angered by this, and insults and confusion ensue. At last things are straightened out when Pickwick and Blotton say they did not intend their remarks in the common sense but in the "Pickwickian sense."

Commentary

The tone of this opening chapter is patronizing, pompous, and tongue-in-cheek. Dickens appears to be satirizing "scientific" clubs, since the object of the Pickwick Club seems to be one of contributing to "scientific" information. Mr. Pickwick, we infer, is a silly old fool surrounded by worshipful admirers. His paper on the Hampstead Ponds and tittlebats is absurd, one assumes, because the title is absurd.

Mr. Pickwick is full of self-congratulation in assuming that his work will benefit humanity and in exaggerating the dangers he will face in traveling. His benign aplomb is shaken, however, when Blotton calls him a humbug. A name-calling session ensues, which effectively destroys any pretense Mr. Pickwick may have had to scientific objectivity. His good humor is restored only when Blotton flatters him by saying that he meant "humbug" in a Pickwickian sense. "Pickwickian sense" is harmless nonsense, a means of retreating from an angry statement, yet it suggests the clubbish atmosphere and Mr. Pickwick's patriarchal role in the club.

Another element of this chapter is worth looking into — the aspect of boyishness. A club like this, all male, usually produces a resurgence of the boyhood spirit, somewhat as fraternities do. It is a snug refuge away from feminine influence, a place where men can be themselves and allow the boy in them free expression. This spirit continues unimpaired through the greater part of the novel, until prison and romance become prominent. Boyishness is stated as one of Tupman's traits, but it is also evident in the foolish title of Mr. Pickwick's paper, in the assumption that scientific doodling is of great importance, in the pompous and cumbersome initials attached to each name, in the appending of inappropriate interests to the main members (which is like calling a fat boy "Slats"), in Mr. Pickwick getting up on his chair to make a speech, in the vainglorious speech, in the name-calling that follows, and in the making-up. So far Mr. Pickwick's childish innocence has been emphasized, but his better qualities will emerge later.

Most of all, though, there is something callow in the inflated, condescending, facetious style of the chapter, which superficially mimics the minutes of a club. One suspects that this was an attempt on Dickens' part (he was twenty-four when he began writing *Pickwick Papers*) to enter into the spirit of the Pickwick Club, to project its jejune tone. In his heavy-handedness we recognize that Dickens is but one step removed from the silly behavior of his characters. However, none of this is out of keeping with the youthful sense of fun that pervades the novel.

CHAPTERS 2-4

Summary

Mr. Pickwick rises at dawn in an exuberant mood and prepares for his first trip. While riding in a cab to meet his friends he takes notes on the cab-driver's fabrications about the horse. The cabbie thinks Mr. Pickwick is an informer, and on reaching the destination he rapidly strikes all the Pickwickians and arouses a crowd against them. However, they are rescued by a self-possessed and seedy young man with a glib line of patter. The stranger joins them on their journey to Rochester and regales them with outlandish impromptu anecdotes about his vast experience.

At Rochester the Pickwickians stop at a fashionable inn and invite the stranger to dinner. Everyone drinks a great deal, and all but Tracy Tupman and the stranger pass out. A dance is underway and Tupman loans the stranger Winkle's dress coat. During the ball the stranger wins a wealthy middle-aged widow away from Dr. Slammer, a local army man. Infuriated, Slammer vows to take revenge.

The next morning a lieutenant looks for the man with Winkle's coat and finds Winkle, whom he challenges to a duel on Slammer's behalf. Winkle is unable to recall anything, but he fearfully accepts the challenge because he has his reputation to keep up. That evening, with Snodgrass as his willing second, Winkle goes to meet Slammer and fully expects to be shot. At the last moment Slammer calls off the duel because he sees that Winkle is the wrong man, and the two men part amiably.

Winkle and Snodgrass return to the inn to find Mr. Pickwick and Tupman with the stranger and a friend of his—a shabby, emaciated actor called "Dismal Jemmy." The actor tells a story about an alcoholic pantomimist who beats his wife and son, goes from bad to worse acting jobs until he is unable to support himself, is forced back on his wife's care, and dies insane.

When the tale is finished the group is interrupted by the arrival of Dr. Slammer and two companions. Recognizing Tupman and the stranger, Slammer demands an explanation. Angry remarks follow, and Slammer and his friends leave with some cutting insults. Mr. Pickwick rushes at them in a fury, but he is restrained by his companions. Soon brandy restores equanimity to the group.

The Pickwickians go to nearby Chatham to see the army maneuvers and are buffeted by the crowd, fired on by the militia, and caught among several regiments in mock-combat. They disentangle themselves to find Mr. Wardle, a country squire, and his family. Wardle invites them to share in the picnic. And while Snodgrass is attracted to Wardle's daughter, Emily, Tupman becomes enamored of Wardle's spinster sister, Rachael, who is jealous of her two attractive nieces. The pleasant outing ends at sunset with Mr. Wardle inviting the Pickwickians to his farm at Dingley Dell.

Commentary

These chapters begin to delineate the Pickwickians by showing them in action. They are out of the cozy club atmosphere and on their own in the world at large. Mr. Pickwick's innocence is dramatized by the fact that he cannot see through the remarks of the cabman or the stranger. His followers are just as inexperienced. The stranger tells an absurd anecdote to each of them that deals with their special field of interest, and they are taken in. The comedy here rests on the exposure of pretensions. But the stranger has pretensions of his own to large possessions, a fat bankroll, wide experience, amorous conquests, and encyclopedic knowledge. The difference is that the stranger is fully aware of his pretenses, and as a result he has perfect self-possession despite his seediness. He can afford his grand, theatrical make-believe because he has nothing to lose by it. Yet the Pickwickians, who have their individual reputations to keep up, are subjected to embarrassments.

This is the point of Winkle accepting Slammer's challenge to duel even though he has no recollection of the insult, and of his doing everything possible to prevent the duel. Winkle must accept because he is a sportsman, and he must get out of it because he has no skill with a gun. The stranger, though, just brushes off Slammer's challenge with an impertinence. The humor lies in Winkle's appeal to Snodgrass to get him out of his predicament, which has to be indirect to keep up appearances, and in Snodgrass' willingness to go through with the duel because a duel is "poetic." Two reputations are at stake. This situation could be grim, except that we know Slammer would not recognize Winkle. Thus potential tragedy is converted into the comedy of discomfiture. This, incidentally, is not the last time Winkle will inadvertently get into trouble over a middle-aged woman.

Each Pickwickian is suffering from a hangover when "Dismal Jemmy" appears with his tale about the alcoholic pantomimist. His story shows a world that is antithetical to comedy, a world where the relations between people are fearful, vicious, and paranoid, where family ties are tenuous, and where the literary style is lurid and melodramatic, like Poe at his worst. Dickens uses the story to show the dark side of alcohol and balances this against the light, comic side of liquor at the chapter's end, where it soothes everyone after the fight with Slammer. Dickens celebrates drinking despite hangovers and alcoholism—it fosters comradeship and good feeling.

Still another contrast is implicit between the stroller's tale and the Pickwickian world, that between viciousness and innocence. The drunkard of the tale is a calamitous father, while Mr. Pickwick is fatherly and protective toward all of his companions, and he is ready to fight when they are insulted. John, the drunkard, is self-destructive, but Mr. Pickwick continues on his innocent, fatherly way. Comedy implies survival.

This chapter also presents another pairing of opposites, which prepares us for the next chapter—the Pickwick group and the army group consisting of the covetous Slammer, the trouble-making Payne and the officious Tappleton. These army men are anti-Pickwickian, motivated by base instincts, ready for trouble, and yet with a clubbish solidarity. In just two chapters Dickens defines the Pickwickians against an adventurer, the stroller's tale, and army clubbism. There is real concentration beneath the diffuse, episodic surface of comedy.

In Chapter 4 Dickens measures the Pickwickians against an anonymous crowd of onlookers, against the anonymous army regiments (both of which threaten their limbs and lives), and then he lets them find their true element in the hospitality and rich life of the Wardles. The Pickwickians stand out from both the anarchic mob of onlookers and the precision of army maneuvers. In the Pickwick Club there is coherence but everyone can maintain his own individuality. The coherence is based on boyish innocence, which is inimical to mob assimilation or army standardization. That these two elements are presented together and threaten the Pickwickians equally shows a remarkable dramatic intuition on Dickens' part.

After their rough exposure to hostile forces, the Pickwickians find a congenial group with which to mix; and the two groups pair off beautifully: Pickwick and Wardle, Tupman and Rachael, Snodgrass and Emily. From the haven of Wardle's barouche the army maneuvers become a pleasant diversion from courting and picnicking. Mr. Wardle has room for everybody—even for Joe the Fat Boy, who is useless, greedy, and somnolent. We have a glimpse of life as a feast, a place where one's trials are rewarded. The invitation to the Wardle farm, in fact, is like an invitation to a terrestial heaven.

In these three chapters, which take us out into the fresh air of the open road, the heaviness which marks the first chapter is dissipated in a style that is colloquial and vivacious. Mr. Pickwick remains somewhat undeveloped, and a jarring note occurs when he approves, in his notebook, of a soldier who wounded a barmaid when she refused to serve him any more liquor and who goes back the next day ready to overlook the incident. This sentiment, while opposed to benevolence, is characteristic of boyhood. One senses that Dickens is feeling his way with Pickwick, but at this point Pickwickianism is a larger reality than Mr. Pickwick.

CHAPTERS 5-7

Summary

Mr. Pickwick rises early and walks to Rochester Bridge, where he meets "Dismal Jemmy" contemplating suicide, or so he says. Jemmy promises to send Mr. Pickwick a manuscript, and Pickwick returns to eat breakfast and prepare for the visit to Wardle's farm. The Pickwickians obtain a chaise, but the inexperienced Winkle must ride horseback. The horses prove unruly, and Winkle loses his while Tupman and Snodgrass are overturned. After trying unsuccessfully to get rid of a horse, the four men arrive at Wardle's bruised and disgruntled. But Mr. Wardle sees that they are cleaned up and given brandy, which refreshes them.

The Pickwickians are introduced to Mr. Wardle's crotchety, cherished, slightly deaf mother and to several neighbors present. The gathering settles down to a card party. Mr. Pickwick and the old lady trounce two neighbors at whist; and the other card table, which is full of young people, is merry and playful. When the card games are finished the local minister is invited to recite a poem about the ivy and how it thrives on decay. That done, the minister is requested by Mr. Wardle to tell the story of "The Convict's Return," in which John Edmunds, a man with a brutal father and a devoted mother, is convicted of theft and serves fourteen years. When he is released he returns home to find his mother dead and his father in a workhouse. Edmunds and his father get into a violent fight, during which the evil father dies of a burst blood vessel. Edmunds then lives repentantly until his death. When the story is finished everyone retires.

Mr. Pickwick gets up early and sees Wardle ready to go crow hunting with Winkle. A group assembles, and Winkle is fearful of his lack of skill—in fact, he shoots Tupman in the arm. Tupman is carried back and greeted by the hysterical Rachael. The Pickwickians leave Tupman in Rachael's care and go with Wardle to nearby Muggleton to see a cricket match. There they meet the glib stranger again, who introduces himself as Alfred Jingle and who is on familiar terms with the All-Muggleton team. The Dingley Dell team is badly beaten, which means they must buy dinner for the winners. Under the influence of alcohol any ill-feeling between the two groups is lost, and everyone stays up drinking until the morning hours.

Commentary

These chapters proceed by means of contrast to show how pleasant life is at Wardle's Manor Farm. In Chapter 5 the suicidal remarks of "Dismal Jemmy" and the difficulties of getting to Wardle's farm make the arrival seem all the more of a blessing. In Chapter 6 the minister's gloomy poem and tale set the attention paid to old Mrs. Wardle and the jollity of cards into relief. In Chapter 7 the wounding of Tupman simply places Tupman where he wants to be—at home with the ladies, who fuss over him. Further, the rather dangerous sport of hunting is contrasted with the team sport of cricket, which in turn leads to a communal feast and late carousing in Muggleton. The Wardle home is capacious, fun-loving, and full of diversions for everyone.

So far Chapters 2, 5, and 7 have begun with Mr. Pickwick getting up with the sun in a buoyant mood. According to the old theory of "humors" Mr. Pickwick embodies the sanguine personality, whose element is fire. He has a sunny disposition; he "beams"; he is hot-tempered: one cannot discuss him without some metaphors of fire, light, and heat creeping in. The sun and the light it casts provides the atmosphere of comedy; and Mr. Pickwick will come to be the warm, radiating center of comedy in this novel.

Balanced against this daylight world, Dickens shows us a night world in the tale and talk of "Dismal Jemmy" and in the tale of the clergyman about John Edmunds. Self-destruction seems to be the main theme of this night world, with revenge as an auxiliary theme. Again, the relation between father and son is brutal, and again the woman is a victim. The savagery of this tale would appall us if it were not safely bracketed as a story. But as part of a tradition of evening storytelling it points up the coziness and good fellowship of the Wardle household, where the old mother is pampered and everyone generally likes everyone else. Dickens uses this contrasting principle throughout the novel. The darkness of the interpolated tale makes the rest of the narrative seem somewhat brighter than it is.

Another feature of these chapters is Dickens' ability to invest animals and minor characters with a personality of their own. The two horses that Pickwick and Winkle take are both ornery and dangerous, but they are ornery in different ways. And a neighbor of Mr. Wardle's, Mr. Miller, has a penchant for putting his foot in his mouth and for losing at whist. Dickens' talent for invention, for getting fun out of things that resist comedy, is very rare, but it gives *Pickwick Papers* a rich and inexhaustible sense of vitality. One can still enjoy this novel after many readings because of Dickens' fertile, life-giving imagination.

CHAPTERS 8-10

Summary

Left at Wardle's, Tupman takes Rachael to a bower and declares his love to her. He is seen kissing her by Joe the Fat Boy. Late that night Wardle and the rest come home from the cricket match hopelessly intoxicated, bringing Jingle with them. Jingle, with his appearance of sobriety, makes a favorable impression on the spinster Rachael. The next day Joe reports Tupman's romance to old Mrs. Wardle, who becomes indignant, and Jingle overhears. Assuming that Rachael has money, Jingle tells her that Tupman is a greedy deceiver. He also tells Tupman that he should ignore Rachael, since he has been discovered, and he borrows ten pounds from Tupman. Thus, Jingle easily replaces Tupman as Rachael's suitor.

A few days later Jingle elopes with Rachael Wardle, and Mr. Wardle is furious. Mr. Pickwick resolves to go along with Wardle to save his sister from an unhappy marriage. After obtaining a chaise, being misled by a bribed gatekeeper, and delayed at an inn in changing horses, they learn that Jingle is directly ahead and charge on through the night. They are about to catch Jingle when a wheel falls off their chaise, which puts a temporary halt to the pursuit. Jingle utters some impertinent remarks from his carriage and drives on gaily, while Wardle and Pickwick are forced to walk.

Sam Weller is blacking boots in the courtyard of the White Hart Inn in London, and Alfred Jingle asks him the way to the Doctors' Commons for a marriage license. Sam then tells him of his father, who was taken in by a marriage license tout and married to a widow that he had no intention of wedding. Jingle purchases the license; and Wardle meanwhile arrives at the inn with his lawyer, Mr. Perker, and with Mr. Pickwick. They learn from Sam Weller where Jingle is staying and confront him in the room with Rachael, who tries to throw a fit. Mr. Perker suggests that Wardle compromise with Jingle, since Rachael is over legal age. So, for 120 pounds Wardle buys Jingle off. Jingle, on leaving, enrages Mr. Pickwick with an impudent gibe about "Tuppy," and Pickwick hurls an inkstand at him. Mr. Pickwick and Mr. Wardle then return to Manor Farm with the humiliated Rachael.

Commentary

This section centers on Jingle's blithe rascality in defaming Tupman, courting Rachael Wardle for her money, eloping with her, and accepting Mr. Wardle's bribe of 120 pounds—eight of which Jingle claims are for his loss of honor and the loss of Rachael!

A number of things take place in these chapters which are of interest. Although Winkle was horror-stricken when he shot Tupman, he comes home drunk that night and says he wishes he had "done for old Tupman," that is, finished him off, which reminds us that Winkle still holds a grudge against Tupman for loaning Jingle his coat, which involved him in the duel. But the remark foreshadows the fact that things are going to go against Tupman.

Chapter 8 shows Tracy Tupman as a ridiculous lover—ridiculous because his girth and age are inappropriate to the kind of passion he exhibits, which would be fitting in a young stage lover. However, Rachael is equally absurd in her coquetry and in falling for Jingle, who is half her age. The fact that Tupman and Rachael can be tricked by an age-old theatrical ploy on Jingle's part means that their feelings were never very deep, and that Tupman was more interested in romantic posturing than in winning Rachael. As a ladies' man Tupman is deservedly a failure. Dickens takes love seriously, and Tupman does not: because of this he is the least sympathetic Pickwickian.

Chapter 9, which depicts the pursuit of Jingle, is quite exhilarating to read. Dickens captures the spirit of the chase in a rapid narrative prose punctuated by breathless dialogue and lively yells to urge on the horses. Even Jingle's swift, stenographic gibes add to the effect. Yet Dickens invents — on the fly as it were — a curmudgeonly gatekeeper who comes alive instantaneously in his sly, ill-tempered remark to himself, where we learn Jingle has bribed him.

In Chapter 10 Dickens gives life to two new characters, each of whom plays an important part in the rest of the book: Sam Weller and Mr. Perker, the lawyer. Sam is a cockney "boots" with charm, worldly wisdom, a wry wit, and curiosity. Sam, like Dickens, has the power to invest people with life by means of anecdote, and we get an accurate, vital picture of Sam's father, Tony, before he makes his appearance. Mr. Perker is a small, lively man with much caution, since he knows the legal dangers of every situation. But he tends to trip up over his own prudence. When he questions Sam about Jingle's whereabouts he gets nowhere, because Sam is equally adept at verbal equivocation.

Something has happened to Mr. Pickwick's psyche in these chapters: he has lost some of his innocence and learned that not everyone is trustworthy. He has also learned that schemers can profit from wrongdoing. Prior to this the comedy was all farcical, a matter of mishaps and misunderstandings, but with Mr. Pickwick's new knowledge the comedy starts to get deeper. Mr. Pickwick is now provided with a motive force, to thwart schemers. Jingle's taunt about "Tuppy" was the last straw.

CHAPTERS 11-12

Summary

On returning to Manor Farm, Mr. Pickwick learns that Tupman has left, intending to commit suicide in a fit of romantic despair. The Pickwickians take their leave of the Wardles and hurry after Tupman, whom they find in Cobham enjoying a hearty meal. Things are patched up, and Mr. Pickwick tells his friends that they will all go to Eatanswill in a few days to witness an election. At Cobham, meanwhile, Mr. Pickwick finds a stone with a strange inscription, which he assumes to be ancient.

Unable to sleep that evening, Mr. Pickwick reads a manuscript that the old clergyman at Wardle's had given him. This story, told in the first person by a raving maniac, relates how the mad author married a woman who was in love with someone else. Her family had contrived the match because the madman was wealthy. He tries to murder his wife because she does not love him, but he is prevented. His wife, however, is driven mad and dies. Her brother, who benefited from the evil marriage, visits the madman and they get into a violent fight, which is interrupted by a crowd of people. The madman, pursued by the crowd, is finally caught and locked in an asylum.

The Pickwickians return to London with the inscribed stone, which everyone makes much of but no one understands. Blotton, a club member, deciphers it accurately as "BILL STUMPS, HIS MARK." But he is expelled and no one pays him any heed.

At his London apartments Mr. Pickwick tells his widowed landlady, Mrs. Bardell, that he has something important to discuss with her. His way of broaching the subject leads her to assume that he is proposing, whereupon she flings her arms about his neck and faints with tearful joy. The three Pickwickians enter at that point, along with Mrs. Bardell's son, Tommy, who starts kicking and butting Mr. Pickwick for hurting his mother. Tupman, Snodgrass, and Winkle look abashed, each assuming that their leader has been up to something. Then Sam Weller enters, and Mr. Pickwick engages Sam, at two suits and 12 pounds a year, to attend on him as a personal servant. This was what Mr. Pickwick wanted to discuss with Mrs. Bardell — whether she could put up Sam Weller.

Commentary

A look at the time scheme up to this point will be helpful. Chapter 1 takes place on May 12, 1827, and the adventures begin on May 13, 1827. By Dickens' own account Chapters 2 to 11 require no more than two weeks, but in Chapter 11 we learn that the trip to Cobham takes place in June. This loose construction of time continues through the novel. In the reading we have the swiftly moving sensation of day-to-day events, largely on Dickens' own clues, but some dates seem out of keeping with normal time logic. Time here is more attuned to dreams than to chronology, and at one point we wonder what happened with time in Chapter 2, where Jingle talks about the July Revolution in 1827 and Dickens says in a footnote that the revolution occurred in 1830. He is warning us not to take time too seriously, that it can be played with like any other element in fiction. This sort of playfulness was something that Sterne had made use of earlier.

After the excitement of the preceding action, Chapter 11 comes as a disappointment: in it Dickens' imagination seems to falter. He reverts to the heavy-handed humor of Chapter 1 in telling of Mr. Pickwick's foolish antiquarian discovery. Blotton, in debunking the great find, is cast as the truth-telling, unpopular club member for the second time, for which he is expelled as a spoilsport. Happily, Dickens has gotten the idea of the Pickwick Club as a scientific club out of his system, so that the humor of the club as a society of friends can flow unimpeded.

The business about Tupman's melodramatic suicide note and his departure — only to be found eating a large meal — simply confirms what we already know of him: that he is a poseur. His romantic pose in the note covers up the fact that he is really running away from possible ridicule.

For all its sensational violence, the madman's tale is a concocted piece of paranoia. Family ties in this story are unscrupulous or murderous. Whereas Wardle has just undertaken a trip to save his sister from a loveless marriage and has paid handsomely to do so, the girl's family in the story is greedy enough to sell her to a lunatic. And her brother, with his false honor, is slightly less repulsive than the madman. It is peculiar that two of the most repugnant tales in the book were told by a benevolent old clergyman at Wardle's. He seems to be a cheerful man with an imagination like "Dismal Jemmy's."

In Chapter 12 Dickens recovers his customary verve in showing how Mr. Pickwick unwittingly leads Mrs. Bardell on. The whole chapter might have been lifted from the popular theater, from which Dickens drew a great deal of inspiration. Misunderstandings like this are part of an ancient stage tradition and are a prominent part of today's situation comedies. The old bachelor who talks in circumlocutions and the marriage-minded, self-deceiving widow are time-honored figures of farce. The further misunderstandings of Tommy Bardell and Mr. Pickwick's friends compound the original error. Moreover, the chapter title tells us that further complications will result.

But Dickens gives the situation an interesting twist. He does not let us know what Mr. Pickwick has in mind until Mrs. Bardell leaves, so that we, too, suspect he may be proposing to her. Thus we become participants in the misunderstanding.

Dickens then introduces a fresh element into the comedy with Sam Weller. When Mr. Pickwick begins beating about the bush with

Sam — the same habit that misled Mrs. Bardell — Sam tells him to come to the point, and their transaction is quickly concluded. Sam will take over the function Blotton had — that of telling the truth; but he will be pleasant and witty about it, revealing the truth by means of apt, impromptu analogies and anecdotes.

Why should Dickens have Mr. Pickwick employ Sam at this point? For one thing, Sam has what Mr. Pickwick lacks: experience of the world. After learning that rascals can flourish, Mr. Pickwick, we assume, realizes that he needs some kind of protection against them. He needs a personal ally in the ensuing adventures, someone who can spot chicanery. Beyond this, Sam will provide a kind of measuring stick against which we can see Mr. Pickwick's personal growth. Sam in his capacity as a servant becomes, as it were, the practical extension of Mr. Pickwick's will. The relationship between the two becomes richer and more intimate as the novel progresses.

By the end of Chapter 12 the mechanics of the plot for the rest of the book have been set in motion.

CHAPTERS 13-14

Summary

At Eatanswill a noisy, contentious election is taking place between the Blues and the Buffs. Each party does its utmost to frustrate and harass the opposition. The Pickwickians arrive in the middle of a shouting contest between a mob of Blues and a mob of Buffs, and Mr. Pickwick tells his companions to yell with the largest mob.

The Pickwickians locate Mr. Perker, now an election adviser for the Blues. Perker tells them about the underhanded tactics of both parties to gain votes, and he introduces them to the editor of the Blue paper, a pompous windbag named Mr. Pott, who invites Pickwick and Winkle to stay at his home. They accept and find that Mrs. Pott treats her husband with condescending sarcasm. Mr. Pott forces Mr. Pickwick to listen to old editorials, while Mrs. Pott takes an interest in young Winkle.

The next morning election excitement is at fever pitch. As the two men prepare for the day's events, Sam Weller tells Mr. Pickwick of how his coachman-father dumped a group of voters in a canal. The Pickwickians are in the Blue procession, which is roughed up by the Buffs.

40

After the Blue candidate, Samuel Slumkey, shakes hands and kisses babies, the nominating and polling procedures get under way amid a deafening hubbub. There is a tie between Samuel Slumkey and his Buff opponent, Horatio Fizkin, which is resolved in Slumkey's favor when Mr. Perker bribes a final group of electors.

In the "commercial room" at the Peacock Inn at Eatanswill, Snodgrass and Tupman become interested in an argument about women, which induces a one-eyed bagman to tell a story about Tom Smart, a poor commercial traveler. Smart is caught in a terrible storm on the heath and barely manages to reach an inn, which is owned by a buxom widow. Tom Smart finds things extremely pleasant there, except for a tall man who is courting the widow. Smart covets the inn and the widow, and goes to bed drunk and disgruntled. He is awakened by an old chair that assumes the features of a sly, elderly man and that tells him how to get rid of the tall man, who is a scoundrel. The next morning Smart finds an incriminating letter, which he shows to the widow, who then decides to marry him. The bagman's listeners remain skeptical.

Commentary

These two chapters contrast the frenetic exertions of an election with the relaxation to be had in a bar with an experienced storyteller. Dickens' coverage of the election is rendered in a coy, ironic prose that exposes the silliness of the event while pretending to take it at its face value. And in the following chapter the style is easy-going, colloquial, conversational, and it captures the moods of a hotel bar gathering especially well. The two prose styles are wonderfully balanced and show Dickens' growing finesse with prose.

The main point about the election is that there are no real issues, merely a lot of commotion, rudeness, and trickery. The two parties are identical; there is no choice or meaning in the election. Slumkey and Fizkin are like Tweedledum and Tweedledee. This fact makes all the passion and violence, all the chicanery and flattery, absurd. The ridiculousness of the event is epitomized when one of Slumkey's committeemen addresses a group of young boys as "men of Eatanswill" and delivers an oration.

At one point Dickens reveals another aspect of Mr. Pickwick's character—his gallantry. When Mrs. Pott waves to him from a rooftop he waves a kiss to her, which the crowd interprets as lechery. Mr. Pickwick becomes indignant, not because of the vulgar remarks about himself, but because Mrs. Pott's honor is slandered. In details like this Dickens is building up a complex and appealing portrait of Mr. Pickwick.

However, Mrs. Pott's honor is rather flexible. She has taken a romantic interest in Winkle and spends much of her time with him — an interest that Winkle will have cause to regret. There is no compatability between her and Mr. Pott. If he is a public lion, he is also a domestic mouse. Mr. Pott habitually talks an editorial jargon, as if he were addressing a crowd. One can understand Mrs. Pott's scorn for him and her regard for young Winkle. The themes of henpecking and cuckolding are an ancient source of humor, probably because men have always viewed women as the weaker sex. However, Winkle is innocent. Dickens could only go so far in suggesting impropriety, but the theme of henpecking will recur several times.

The bagman's tale is perfect for a "commercial room" (hotel bar) and an all-male audience, since it assumes women are fair game, it has a leering shrewdness, and it shows how a little fellow triumphs over his flashier and taller rival. Tupman, who hears the story, must have been quite receptive to it after the rascally Jingle had just taken Rachael from him. Another contrast is implicit in this tale, which depicts a widow as being a defenseless, amiable prey for a man with pluck. In the novel widows are predatory, while men are the defenseless victims.

Time is given a severe wrench in Chapter 13, where Mr. Pott pulls out his files for 1828 to read two-year-old editorials to Mr. Pickwick. At Cobham in June, 1827, Mr. Pickwick said the group would go to Eatanswill in a few days; and here three years have vanished. In this novel time has its warps and lapses, much as it does in surrealist literature.

CHAPTERS 15-17

Summary

Still at Eatanswill, the Pickwickians are invited to a costume breakfast by Mrs. Leo Hunter, a wretched poetess who seeks celebrated acquaintances and who sends her husband as an errand-boy. Mr. Pickwick gets furious when Tupman says he plans to dress, inappropriately, as a bandit. But the quarrel is smoothed over, and the Pickwickians turn up at Mrs. Leo Hunter's party. The place is full of poseurs — minor celebrities dressed as they would like to appear but simply parading their silliness. Count Smorltork has a tenuous, malapropian grasp of English but he considers himself an expert on English life after a two-week visit. Alfred Jingle turns up disguised as a Mr. Fitz-Marshall, and he makes a hasty exit when he encounters Mr. Pickwick, who chases him to Bury St. Edmunds in order to expose him.

Mr. Pickwick and Sam Weller arrive at Bury St. Edmunds and go to a large inn, the Angel. The next morning Sam meets Jingle's servant, Job Trotter, a cadaverous, tearful man. Job tells Sam of his master's scheme to elope with a rich girl in a nearby boarding school. Job Trotter then suggests a plan to Mr. Pickwick by which the girl can be saved. This involves Mr. Pickwick's waiting in the boarding school garden to surprise Jingle in the act. Mr. Pickwick acts accordingly and is caught in a terrible storm. He can only escape the storm by entering the boarding school, which is full of hysterical women. The women lock him in a closet full of sandwich bags, and he asks them to send for his servant, Sam, who arrives later with Mr. Wardle and Mrs. Trundle. Wardle is in the area on a hunting expedition, and he accidentally learned of Mr. Pickwick's presence. The trouble is straightened out; but that night Mr. Pickwick and Sam vow to get even with Jingle and Job Trotter for that trick.

Laid up with rheumatism for a few days, Mr. Pickwick manages to recover his good spirits. At the hotel he relates the tale of the parish clerk to Wardle and Trundle. A provincial schoolmaster named Nathaniel Pipkin falls in love with pretty Maria Lobbs and with her father's money. Maria teases him but without any romantic intent. She invites him to tea at her house when her terrible-tempered father, Old Lobbs, is absent. Maria's handsome cousin, Henry, is also at the party, and Nathaniel becomes jealous when he notices Maria's interest in her cousin. Old Lobbs returns and Henry and Nathaniel are hidden in closets, but they are discovered. Maria pleads for Henry, who shows himself to be honorable, and Old Lobbs consents to the marriage. The frustrated Nathaniel runs amok on the wedding day.

Commentary

These chapters center on knaves and fools, rascals and fakes. Mr. Pickwick, having learned that dishonesty exists and that it can prosper, begins a career of combating it. Dishonesty begins appearing everywhere in various forms, from the pretenses of the costume party, to Jingle's alias, to Job Trotter's practical joke, to certain aspects of the interpolated tale. Mr. Pickwick, while he may be taken in by trickery, stands apart from it. And he finds an ally in Sam Weller to help him expose it.

Mrs. Hunter's party is a social error, since the idea of a costume breakfast is absurd. Costume parties are held at night, not in glaring daylight. Further, the costumes that the characters choose reveal their aspirations, which are out of keeping with their real nature. Tupman goes as a romantic stage bandit, although he is fat and fiftyish. Snodgrass goes as a troubadour, but he cannot write verse. Winkle dresses as a sportsman, though he has no coordination. The disgruntled housewife, Mrs. Pott, goes as the sun god Apollo. The browbeaten Mr. Pott goes as a fierce Russian judge. The simple-minded Mrs. Leo Hunter postures as the intellectual Minerva. To complete the absurdity, the costumes themselves are totally inaccurate.

Pretense, of course, is the key to Mrs. Leo Hunter's circle. Mr. Pickwick is the only one who wears his normal dress. He is incapable of imposture, and he dislikes it in his companion, Tupman, when it verges on the ridiculous. However, his companions are too absorbed in their roles to follow his example.

Dickens, incidentally, uses names to reveal a character's function. *Leo Hunter* means lion hunter, one who seeks celebrities. *Count Smorltork*, who mangles everyone's name, has a distorted phrase for a name: small talk.

The principal impostor at the party is Alfred Jingle, who uses the alias, Charles Fitz-Marshall. Amid the toadying and pretense he enters his true element. The party is a milieu where a person can be anything he chooses, where character is fluid and amorphous. However, Jingle cannot enjoy this freedom long because he is recognized and frightened off by the one real person there, Mr. Pickwick.

From the humbug of Eatanswill society Dickens moves to the budding friendship between Mr. Pickwick and Sam Weller. Chapter 16 begins with Pickwick and Sam pleasantly conversing on master-and-servant terms to while away the journey to Bury St. Edmunds; and it ends with Sam vowing to aid Mr. Pickwick in chastising Jingle and Job Trotter. Sam, as well as Mr. Pickwick, is fooled by Job Trotter, which wounds his pride. In this way Sam becomes involved in Mr. Pickwick's emotional life: they share the humiliation of the practical joke. They are still technically master and servant, but a big change has taken place. Both men have taken a protective interest in each other. They are now confederates.

Although he has a debilitating attack of rheumatism, Mr. Pickwick recovers his good spirits and sense of humor soon after the incident.

Comedy depends upon the resilience of human nature, the ability to bounce back after serious setbacks. Comedy requires a sense of proportion, above all — the commonplace knowledge that one or two disappointments are not the end of the world.

The tale that Mr. Pickwick relates to Wardle and Trundle is rather light-hearted. Dickens borrowed the idea from Washington Irving's *The Legend of Sleepy Hollow*, but it fits its setting in the novel. The theme of deception is very prominent. Nathaniel Pipkin thinks he wants Maria Lobbs but really covets her father's money and power. Maria Lobbs leads him on, but she actually loves her cousin. The game of blindman's buff at her party symbolizes Nathaniel's mental blindness. He is a butt who gets what he deserves. His mercenary intent is very similar to Jingle's, and the fact that Pipkin gets nothing probably soothes Mr. Pickwick's feelings after being outsmarted. A further irony is that Old Lobbs is a literary caricature of Wardle, who hears the tale.

CHAPTERS 18-19

Summary

Winkle, who has stayed on for a few days with the Potts, is confronted one morning with a raging Mr. Pott. A poem has appeared in the opposition paper that accuses Winkle of cuckolding Mr. Pott. Mrs. Pott throws a hysterical fit and pressures her husband into thrashing the editor, Mr. Slurk. Under the circumstances Winkle finds it expedient to leave, and he goes with Tupman and Snodgrass to meet Mr. Pickwick at Bury St. Edmunds. When they arrive they find Mr. Wardle, who extends an invitation to the Pickwickians to visit him at Manor Farm over Christmas, when they will celebrate Trundle's wedding to Isabella Wardle.

Upon learning of Winkle's difficulty at the Potts', Mr. Pickwick delivers a lecture to Tupman and Winkle on the impropriety of causing romantic turmoil when one is a guest. The lecture is interrupted when Mr. Pickwick receives a letter informing him that Mrs. Bardell is suing him for breach of promise. His companions gleefully remind him of the time they found him holding her in his arms, and he is horrified. Mr. Pickwick determines to return to London soon to get legal assistance.

The following day the Pickwickians, Wardle, and Trundle go hunting. Because Mr. Pickwick is still lame with rheumatism he has to be taken in a wheelbarrow. Both Winkle and Tupman are inexperienced and dangerous in handling a gun, for which they are reproved by Mr. Pickwick. However, Tupman shoots a partridge by accident, which gains him the reputation of being a marksman. At length they all have lunch, during which Mr. Pickwick drinks too much and falls asleep. The rest decide to leave him and come back for him later. A bit later the owner of the land, a fierce, belligerent man named Captain Boldwig, comes upon the sleeping Pickwick and has him carted to the animal pound. There a crowd gathers and starts throwing things at Mr. Pickwick, but he is rescued by Mr. Wardle and Sam Weller. His sense of humiliation is gradually overcome by his natural good humor.

Commentary

These chapters finish up the business at Eatanswill and Bury St. Edmunds. Caught between Pott's fury and Mrs. Pott's infatuation, Winkle is forced to leave Eatanswill. And Mr. Pickwick must leave Bury St. Edmunds because of Mrs. Bardell's lawsuit. Both exits are the result of romantic misunderstandings. However, as if to balance this woman trouble, Dickens depicts an all-male hunting party, where he shows the trouble that men can get into on their own.

Dickens' handling of the scene between the Potts and Winkle shows some interesting characterization. Mr. Potts simply cares about the damage to his public image, not about Mrs. Pott's fidelity. What galls him is that Winkle has unwittingly enabled the opposition paper to ridicule him. He makes no distinction between the public accusation and the private reality, since he is merely a public figure in his own eyes. This view of himself leaves him vulnerable to his wife, who can do just as she pleases with him. Hysterics, even when faked, can make him cringe. Throughout the scene Winkle is passive and somewhat astonished at the havoc his presence has caused. In his innocence he shows a gift for stepping into nasty situations.

Mr. Pickwick's lecture to his companions about causing romantic consternation involves two ironies. The first is obvious: he himself has misled Mrs. Bardell, albeit unintentionally. Everyone, including Sam Weller, appears to believe the worst of Mr. Pickwick, which is usually the case if one is innocent. The fact that Mrs. Bardell has started a lawsuit against him shows how serious his inadvertent deception was. With his circumlocutions Mr. Pickwick participated in the very dishonesty he is out to combat. The second irony is that while Mr. Pickwick is addressing his remarks to Winkle and Tupman, Snodgrass is having a clandestine romance with Emily Wardle.

The hunting trip seems like a gratuitous episode that interrupts two emerging plots (getting even with Jingle and Mrs. Bardell's lawsuit), but it is intended to show some of the difficulties men can get into without the help of women. Beyond this it lends a sense of amplitude to the novel.

One difficulty on the hunting trip is that of taking along a lame Pickwick in a wheelbarrow. This is a serious breach of decorum to the gamekeeper, as well as a heavy burden to Sam Weller, who has to push the barrow. The next difficulty lies in the hazardous manner in which Winkle and Tupman carry their guns. As a professed sportsman Winkle is very touchy about being corrected. Sam is forced to needle Winkle in a wryly funny way to make him follow Mr. Pickwick's orders. Then at lunch Mr. Pickwick takes too much punch and falls asleep, which leads to his being left unprotected. This puts him at the mercy of Captain Boldwig, a country squire who acts like a feudal lord and who has him hustled off to the animal pound, where is is pelted with vegetables. These troubles are all temporary, if they are humiliating and worrisome. The difference between romantic difficulties and the problems men create for themselves, Dickens seems to imply, is that romantic difficulties are more serious, more lasting, more dangerous. If Winkle had not left, Pott would have poisoned him. And the Bardell lawsuit will land Mr. Pickwick in prison.

There are other aspects of Chapter 19 that bear attention. Back in Chapter 7 Dickens also poked fun at Winkle's awkwardness with a gun, but there he did it through an ironic narration. Here he employs Sam Weller's gibes, and the effect is more personal and funnier. For example, Sam tells Winkle that if he doesn't stop pointing the gun at his head Winkle will have a full game bag and something to spare. Sam's wit is based on a recognition of the grim facts of life; he gives a humorous twist to unpleasant observations. Sam has become the center of intelligence in the novel, just as Mr. Pickwick has become the center of kindliness.

Dickens creates Captain Boldwig swiftly through the man's orders to servants, his brusque speech rhythms and his prop — the big stick with the brass ferrule. Boldwig, like Wardle, is a hot-tempered country squire. But whereas Wardle is a generous, hospitable, unpretentious man, Boldwig is mean, inhospitable, completely absorbed in his pretentious role of the feudal lord.

Mr. Pickwick has no past for all practical purposes. At the hunting picnic he tries to remember a song from infancy, drinks himself into an infant-like sleep, and is wheeled to the animal pound in his wheel-barrow-perambulator. Dickens intends Mr. Pickwick's life to be co-extensive with the course of the novel. He starts off as innocent as a very young boy and ends wise and mature: this is all we need to see of Mr. Pickwick's life. When an old man can recapture the spirit of infancy or boyhood or youth almost at will, his past becomes irrelevant. In a sense, Mr. Pickwick was born reading his paper about the Hampstead Ponds and tittlebats, just as Stephen Dedalus was born talking about a moocow in *Portrait of the Artist as a Young Man.*

We learn that the dates of these two chapters are August 30-31, Tuesday and Wednesday, in 1830. This very specificity brings us up short because time has been rather vague up to this point. The Pick-wickians have been invited to Wardle's for the Christmas holidays, and from there on time will become less elastic because of the proceedings in the Bardell lawsuit.

CHAPTERS 20-21

Summary

Having arrived in London, Mr. Pickwick goes to Dodson and Fogg's office. While waiting he and Sam overhear the clerks' talk about Fogg and his underhanded practices. On obtaining an interview with the two lawyers, Mr. Pickwick learns to his indignation that the damages are set at 1,500 pounds, and he obtains a copy of the writ against him. Then he and Sam step into a tavern for a drink, and Sam recognizes his father, who joins them. Sam's father tells Mr. Pickwick that he recognized Jingle and Job Trotter on the Ipswich coach, and Mr. Pickwick resolves to pursue them.

Next, Mr. Pickwick and Sam go to Mr. Perker's office to turn over the copy of the writ. No one is there but a charwoman, who tells them that Mr. Perker's clerk is at a nearby tavern. So they go there, hand the clerk the writ, which he promises to take care of, and Mr. Pickwick joins the clerk at his table. The clerk, Peter Lowten, introduces Pickwick to his friends, who are seedy, unkempt law clerks. And Mr. Pickwick settles down to hear some stories about Gray's Inn, which are told by a half-crazed man named Jack Bamber.

Bamber begins by telling of dead bodies and ghosts in the chambers of the Inns of Court. And then with a hideous leer he launches into the tale of the queer client. Imprisoned for debt in the Marshalsea, a man called Heyling watches his wife and child wither and die. He swears to be avenged on the two men who placed him in prison: his father and father-in-law. His father dies, which releases Heyling and makes him rich. One day Heyling finds his brother-in-law drowning while his father-in-law pleads for help, and Heyling lets the man drown. Later Heyling buys up his father-in-law's debts and begins to persecute him legally. Reduced to destitution, the old man flees, but Heyling tracks him down. As the old man sits in his rented room Heyling enters and tells him of his own vow to destroy him, and the old man dies.

After the story Mr. Pickwick pays the bill and leaves.

Commentary

Among other things, these two chapters deal with the law, with how contorted justice can become when the law is used to serve mercenary or evil ends. Dodson and Fogg, of course, are wholly unprincipled. After serving Mr. Pickwick with one misbegotten suit, they try to make him slander or assault them so they can start other suits against him. Moreover, their moral corruption extends to their clerks, who heartily approve of chicanery. Mr. Pickwick finds himself confronted by a new kind of knavery, which is completely distinct from Jingle's flamboyant schemes. Dodson and Fogg are determined and ruthless, and they have the machinery of the law behind them. Jingle has nothing behind him but his own quick wit.

Bamber's tale of the queer client shows how Heyling uses the law to hound a man to his death, after the man had sent him to debtors' prison with the same hardness. Thus law can become the instrument of paranoid cruelty. Dickens shows the law at its shabbiest in the talk and stories of the law clerks, and he clearly has little respect for it. Personal experience may have helped shaped this view, for Dickens was a law clerk for awhile in his teens.

It is no coincidence that Sam's father, Tony Weller, is introduced just after Mr. Pickwick has been handed a breach-of-promise writ. Tony is caught up in a miserable marriage to a widow, and Mr. Pickwick is learning how mercenary a thwarted widow can be. Both men are innocents when it comes to women and are liable to be imposed upon.

The relationship between Tony and Sam is closer to an easy companionship than to a normal father-son relation. Tony exercises no parental authority over Sam, who was put out on the street at an early age to learn the ways of the world on his own. Although Sam has not seen his father in two years, they are on friendly terms. In Bamber's tale the theme of fathers and sons appears as a negative of Sam's filial love for Tony and Mr. Pickwick. Heyling vows to destroy his father and father-in-law, and there is no quarter given on either side.

Tony Weller's information that Jingle and Job Trotter are at Ipswich provides the destination of the next adventure. So far Jingle's itinerary coincides closely with Mr. Pickwick's. Jingle is almost a reverse image of Mr. Pickwick, a shadow self who turns up in the same places and who has acquired a servant simultaneously with Mr. Pickwick. Mr. Pickwick, in fact, is a bit obsessed with Jingle, for he was the one who taught him about the reality and power of deception, and who tripped him up in his own gallantry at Bury St. Edmunds.

Dickens is beginning to weave two separate but related plot lines together: Jingle's schemes to marry money and Mrs. Bardell's plan to get money out of Mr. Pickwick, both of which are underhanded. Mr. Pickwick is fighting his battle against dishonesty on two fronts: he hates to see others cheated and he hates to be cheated himself.

CHAPTERS 22-25

Summary

While loading the coach to Ipswich Mr. Weller tells Sam about the unsavory evangelist with whom his wife had taken up. Mr. Pickwick arrives and gets into conversation with a prissy, conceited man named Peter Magnus, who is also going to Ipswich. When the journey is over Pickwick and Magnus register at a large inn, and Magnus tells Mr. Pickwick that he came to propose to a woman at that inn. That night Mr. Pickwick loses his way while trying to find his room. By mistake he enters the bedroom of a middle-aged woman, undresses, discovers his mistake, throws the lady into a panic, and makes a fumbling exit. He decides to wait in the hallway, where Sam finds him and leads him back to his room. Sam suspects that he has been after the ladies.

The next morning Tony Weller tells Sam that it is a disgrace to the family honor to have been tricked by Job Trotter, and Sam reminds his father of the disgrace of letting an evangelist impose on him. A bit later Sam meets Job Trotter emerging from someone's yard. Job tries to evade him but does not succeed. Sam can extract no information about Jingle from him, but Job tells him that he himself is interested in marrying a

cook for her savings. They part, and Sam tells Mr. Pickwick about a plan
he has in mind.

Mr. Pickwick has breakfast with Peter Magnus, who is very agitated.
Magnus gets Mr. Pickwick's advice on proposing and rushes off. Then
Tupman, Snodgrass, and Winkle arrive. Magnus returns to tell Mr.
Pickwick that the lady has accepted him, and he invites him to meet his
fiancée. She is, of course, the same lady Mr. Pickwick had frightened the
night before. Embarrassment follows, which throws Magnus into a rage.
He threatens to duel with Mr. Pickwick, who seems ready to accept. The
lady, Miss Witherfield, is terrified and reports Mr. Pickwick and Tupman to the local justice, Mr. Nupkins, who has an exaggerated sense of
authority. Mr. Nupkins sends his officers to arrest the two men. After a
good deal of consternation Mr. Pickwick and Tupman agree to go peace-
fully. Sam, on learning of his master's arrest, gets into a fight with the
officers, who manage to subdue him. The Pickwickians are led away to
the justice's, followed by a crowd of onlookers.

Mr. Nupkins conducts the trial in a belligerent, highhanded manner. He fines Snodgrass and Winkle and requires a large bail from Mr.
Pickwick and Tupman. Mr. Pickwick is furious, but after a private talk
with Sam he asks Nupkins for a quiet conference, in which Nupkins
learns that his daughter's fashionable suitor is really the impostor
Jingle. Realizing that this information could cause great social embarrassment for him and his family, Nupkins tells Mr. Pickwick that he can
stay and confront Jingle. On learning the news Mrs. Nupkins and her
daughter berate Mr. Nupkins for their own poor judgment, but they
decide it would be best to send Jingle and his servant off quietly. Sam,
meanwhile, has dinner with the servants and strikes up a romance with
the pretty housemaid, Mary. When Job Trotter turns up the servants are
ready for him, and the cook on whom he had designs rushes at him to
tear his hair out. Jingle remains just as self-possessed as ever upon
being exposed. But when he and Job leave the house they are dumped
into the bushes by the butler. Having accomplished their purpose, Mr.
Pickwick and Sam return to London.

Commentary

These chapters show the circuitous way in which Jingle and Job
Trotter receive their punishment at the hands of Mr. Pickwick and Sam
Weller. Dickens seems to alternate episodes in which the Pickwickians
enjoy a vacationing life with episodes where Mr. Pickwick has some
specific purpose. This alternation between relaxation and effortful

purpose simulates the actual rhythms of life. Plot itself depends on a goal to be reached. A common mistake in looking at *Pickwick Papers* is to take too narrow a view of plot. While Mr. Pickwick may have fits and starts of activity, his adventures are not the plot of the novel. The real plot of the novel lies in Dickens' mental activity, in the way he conceives of Mr. Pickwick's development. *Pickwick Papers* is a comedy of education, after all.

Although Mr. Pickwick is sexually innocent, everyone seems to suspect him of having liaisons with women. The crowd at Eatanswill accused him of it in a bantering way. His closest companions are doubtful of his relationship to Mrs. Bardell. A casual acquaintance, Peter Magnus, not only insinuates it but asks Mr. Pickwick's advice on proposing and flies into a jealous rage later. Even Sam Weller is suspicious when he finds Mr. Pickwick in his nightclothes in the hallway of the inn late at night. At Mr. Pickwick's age this might be flattering. A charming bit of irony occurs when Mr. Pickwick gives Magnus his recipe for proposing, since he is involved in a breach-of-promise suit.

While Mr. Pickwick is the soul of kindness, he is not soft. Where his principles are concerned he has a lot of courage. When he speaks up to Nupkins as he does, he is fully aware of the possible consequences. Injustice is one thing that he cannot abide.

A prominent feature of these chapters is the way in which servants imitate their masters. Job Trotter plans a mercenary marriage with the Nupkins' cook, just as Jingle plans one with their daughter. The police officer, Grummer, borrows Nupkins' inflated authority and his pretense at learning. And while Sam Weller exposes Job Trotter to the Nupkins' servants Mr. Pickwick is exposing Jingle to the Nupkins. In a very tangible sense each master determines the character and bearing of his underling, and the moral quality of the master shows up in the servant.

The master-servant relationship is a variation of the father-son theme. In both cases the principle is the same: persons with less power mimic those with greater power, partly to reduce emotional friction and partly to borrow the power. Here Dickens begins to define Sam's relationship to Mr. Pickwick and Tony Weller more fully. Mr. Pickwick tells Magnus that he allows Sam many liberties (including the right to talk back) because Sam is "an original." He takes a personal pride in Sam. Sam proves his value in this episode when his information leads to Jingle's exposure and to the cancellation of fines and bail. Mr. Pickwick and Sam now share a mutual victory that wipes out their mutual humiliation.

Sam and his father, Tony, are more or less on an equal footing. If Tony can mention Sam's loss of face in being hoodwinked by Job Trotter, Sam can point out Tony's tarnished honor in allowing an evangelist to sponge on him. Nonetheless, the reader can detect a good deal of affection between the two men. Though two years had passed since Sam had seen his father, they are beginning to grow closer now. In fact, in Chapter 27 Sam makes a special trip to see his father in Dorking.

Dickens depicts Sam's relationship to Mr. Pickwick and Tony Weller with warmth and vitality, but Sam's romance with Mary fails to come alive at all. Dickens often seems unable to show a courtship without becoming distastefully cute or maudlin. It may be a wholesome act for Sam to give Mary kisses behind the door on the pretext of looking for a hat, but the way Dickens gloats over it is tiresome. One usually has a distinct sense of uneasiness when Dickens turns to romance. Either through social propriety or deep personal inhibitions, he was frequently unable to give life to a courtship. And while Dickens may have believed in love, he rarely succeeded in portraying it.

CHAPTERS 26-27

Summary

Mr. Pickwick makes arrangements to move out of Mrs. Bardell's house and into a hotel. He sends Sam Weller to pay the rent, give a month's notice, and see about having his possessions moved. Sam is also supposed to find out what is taking place with regard to the lawsuit. Sam's arrival throws Mrs. Bardell and two visiting neighbors into a flurry, but his apparent sympathy invites them to discuss the suit. Sam learns that Mrs. Bardell intends to take Mr. Pickwick to court, and that Dodson and Fogg have a good chance of winning, since they took the case on speculation. Sam reports this to Mr. Pickwick, who is making preparations for his Christmas visit to Dingley Dell.

Sam takes two days leave from Mr. Pickwick to visit his father at Dorking. He finds his stepmother sitting with a seedy gluttonous evangelist, neither of whom is very pleased to see him. The Reverend Stiggins and Susan Weller are self-righteously united against Sam's father, Tony. It is obvious that Stiggins takes advantage of the Wellers. Mr. Weller arrives and greets Sam warmly, and the two of them discuss Stiggins' hypocrisy. Before he leaves the next day Sam tells his father that he would get rid of Stiggins, to which Tony replies that it is one of the burdens of marriage.

Commentary

Sam Weller is the principal character in these two chapters, but he is present mainly as an observer. In the first he learns of Mr. Pickwick's legal situation from Mrs. Bardell and her two neighbors, Mrs. Cluppins and Mrs. Sanders. In the second Sam learns the marital situation of his father at firsthand. The point of these chapters is that both Mr. Pickwick and Mr. Weller are victims of self-deceiving widows, to which the contiguity of these chapters calls attention. Mrs. Bardell tries to make out that her case against Mr. Pickwick is a matter of sentiment, whereas it is really a matter of greed and obtaining revenge. And Mrs. Weller tries to make out that she dislikes her husband on religious principles, but it is actually because she is infatuated with the repulsive Stiggins.

Food and drink play an interesting part here. Sam arrives at Mrs. Bardell's and at Susan Weller's just as food is being prepared by the two widows. At Mrs. Bardell's, Mrs. Cluppins is anxious that Sam leave without eating, while at the Wellers' the Reverend Stiggins openly resents Sam's intrusion at teatime. It is this atmosphere of petty piggishness that is most telling about the widows' friends. Another suggestive detail is that each of these companions has a hypocritical attitude toward liquor, outwardly disdaining it and inwardly relishing it.

Although one could assume from the day-to-day events that this section takes place in September (the adventure at Ipswich takes just a few days and begins early in September), we are informed that the Pickwickians are preparing to go to Wardle's for Christmas. This leads us into the next episode, but like the other time-lapses it gives us a feeling of time's swiftness. The feeling is entirely appropriate to a novel in which good companions and spirited adventures predominate.

CHAPTERS 28-30

Summary

In a holiday mood the Pickwickians take the coach to Muggleton, a ride everyone enjoys. They are met by Joe the Fat Boy, and from Muggleton they walk to the Wardle farm, where they are given a hearty reception. The Wardles are visited by several young women, friends of the Wardle girls, who have come to see Isabella married to Mr. Trundle. Winkle begins a romance with one of the young ladies, Arabella Allen, and Snodgrass is happy to see Emily again. The next couple of days are given over to the marriage and wedding breakfast, to card games, dancing, feasting, drinking and toasts, singing, flirtation, kissing games, and storytelling. Everyone is in the best of spirits.

Full of holiday gaiety, old Mr. Wardle tells the story of the goblins who stole a sexton. Gabriel Grub, a mean, misanthropic sexton, goes to dig a grave on Christmas Eve and beats up a little boy on the way. The work is hard, and when Grub rests to take a drink he meets the king of goblins, who accuses him of being a nasty, spiteful fellow. A short trial follows in which he is condemned by the goblins, who take him to an underground cavern and kick him mercilessly. They also show him scenes of life that exalt goodness, cheer, and beauty. The next morning he arises, a converted man, and leaves the area for ten years. When he returns he is old, poor, but happy, and he tells what had happened to him.

One morning Mr. Pickwick gets up to find two medical students in the Wardle kitchen. Ben Allen and Bob Sawyer are ill-mannered, slovenly, high-spirited young men who, over breakfast, cheerfully talk of dissecting bodies. Winkle enters with his sweetheart, Arabella Allen, who is surprised to see her brother Ben. Winkle is jealous of Bob Sawyer's attentions to Arabella. Everyone goes to church, and afterward a skating party gets underway. Winkle demonstrates his ineptitude. The skaters are full of merriment until Mr. Pickwick falls through the ice. Eventually he is hauled out, and he rushes home to bed, where he drinks a quantity of punch, which saves him from illness. The following morning the festivities break up. Bob Sawyer invites Mr. Pickwick to a party in London; Winkle and Snodgrass take leave of their sweethearts; and the Pickwickians return to London.

Commentary

These chapters are at the very center of the novel in both a literal and figurative sense. They celebrate Christmas, benevolence, gaiety, plenty, and friendship. While Dickens evinces Christian feeling, he has secularized Christmas. Here Christmas is primarily an occasion for a wedding, for large gatherings, for nostalgia and merriment. Its religious core, the birth of Christ, has been removed. What is left then is a multitude of activities and people designed to produce good feeling.

In a similar spirit Isabella Wardle and Mr. Trundle are minor figures at their own wedding, which is viewed as a pretext for celebration. What Dickens wants to capture is the crowd spirit, the group mood to which everyone contributes his own special note. At the heart of this mass festivity is Mr. Pickwick, who almost seems like an allegorical emblem of generosity and good cheer. Opposed to him is the story figure of Gabriel Grub, who stands for meanness and cruelty. But even Grub must yield to the Christmas spirit. In these chapters Dickens lays bare the meaning of his novel in an abstract way. At times his own voice becomes obtrusive, and the characters tend to become symbols.

However, Mr. Pickwick resists Dickens' abstractions; he remains a living character. Women regard him as "an old dear" and they delight in mobbing him and smothering him with kisses during the fun. He is perfectly at ease in their company. Gallant, generous, gentlemanly, Mr. Pickwick is adored by women, even if he does not inspire a romantic interest.

The tale of Gabriel Grub shows a mirror-image not just of Mr. Pickwick but of the action of the whole novel. Grub begins by leading a harsh, constricted, miserable life. He is tried and punished by goblins. And he emerges a reformed man. Mr. Pickwick begins by leading a rambling, adventurous, amiable life. He is tried in court, goes to prison, and comes out a wiser, less exuberant man. He does not lose his benevolence, however. It simply takes a more purposeful form.

One does not object to Dickens' treatment of romance in this section. While Winkle and Arabella and Snodgrass and Emily are hopelessly pallid — deliberate nonentities like Isabella and Trundle — they have their place as romantic figures in the festive background. If Dickens uses a coy tone to portray them, it is kept subordinate to other features.

Bob Sawyer and the doltish Ben Allen are much more vivid after three pages than Winkle and Snodgrass will ever be. One can understand Mr. Pickwick's ready acceptance of an invitation to their party in London despite their boisterous vulgarity and shabbiness.

CHAPTERS 31-33

Summary

One evening in January Dodson and Fogg's clerk, Mr. Jackson, barges into Mr. Pickwick's hotel room, tells him the trial will be held on February 14, and serves Tupman, Snodgrass, Winkle, and Sam with subpoenas to appear as witnesses for Mrs. Bardell. Mr. Pickwick then goes to see his lawyer, Mr. Perker, and learns that his case is doubtful. Pickwick insists on seeing his courtroom attorney, Serjeant Snubbin, a disorderly, untidy man with a big reputation. Mr. Pickwick insists he is innocent of the charge but receives little reassurance from Perker, Snubbin, or Mr. Phunky, who is Snubbin's nervous, self-effacing assistant in the case.

Living in a dismal, impoverished neighborhood, Bob Sawyer is harangued by his vituperative landlady, Mrs. Raddle, because he cannot pay the rent. The Pickwickians arrive at his party, to which a number of medical students have been invited. One named Jack Hopkins relates some lugubrious anecdotes about medical curiosities. The party is a disaster. An angry dispute arises at cards. The dinner is a failure. Sawyer cannot obtain hot water to make drinks. A long, tedious story is told in which the point has been forgotten. Two men are ready to duel. There is no harmony to the singing. And Mrs. Raddle enters the room screaming, which puts an end to the party.

On February 13 Sam Weller writes a valentine to Mary the housemaid, which dismays his father, who thinks Sam should avoid women. Sam is deterred and signs the valentine, "Your love-sick Pickwick." Mr. Weller also thinks that Mr. Pickwick needs an alibi. Tony then invites Sam to a temperance meeting. After much tea is consumed, and after absurd testimonials to the harmfulness of liquor and an equally absurd song, Stiggins enters, drunk and belligerent. He starts fighting and throws the meeting into an uproar. The lights go out and Mr. Weller lands some punches on Stiggins. Sam has to grab his father and the pair make a quick getaway.

Commentary

In these chapters several subjects are treated satirically: the legal and medical professions, aggressive middle-aged women, valentines, and temperance organizations.

Dickens' most serious attack is against the legal profession, which he knew a good deal about. He shows the squalor of its quarters and its practitioners, the callousness of Perker's clerk in shooing away a ragged man, the appreciation Perker has for questionable legal tricks, the extortion practiced by Serjeant Snubbin's well-dressed secretary, Snubbin's habit of obtaining a fee before he does anything, and the general attitude of the profession that law is a game which has nothing to do with morality. The law, in effect, is a machine for putting money into lawyers' pockets.

Dickens pokes fun at the medical profession by depicting the hard-living milieu of medical students, who have no interest in curing people. They respect surgeons like Dr. Slasher, who cuts off a boy's leg as a remedy for a stomach-ache. Doctors seem motivated by sadism and an interest in medical curiosities. Dickens may be wide of the mark in this, but the episode of Bob Sawyer's party is good fun.

Mrs. Raddle is another of the comic, formidable middle-aged women in this book, but she is more hysterical and more aggressive than the others—a real fighter. Her angry calls to her husband, trying to get him to assist her in throwing out the medical students, are a pretext for demeaning his masculinity. She needs no help and she knows it, but she enjoys the pretense of exasperated helplessness. It is her only connection to femininity.

Sam Weller reminds the reader that the date of Mr. Pickwick's trial is Valentine's Day, the irony being that the trial is for breach of promise. His own valentine to Mary is a comic masterpiece. The crowning touch is the signature, as if to embroil Mr. Pickwick in more difficulties. The scene in which Sam reads the letter to his father is remarkably charming.

The temperance meeting is broad farce with a satirical intent. Dickens hated sanctimonious Puritanism all his life and enjoyed making fun of it. The humor of the meeting rests in its incongruities. Sam and Tony Weller have had plenty to drink before they go. The audience drinks large amounts of tea, which acts as a stimulant. The speakers are pious frauds. The testimonials are of dubious value. The song is a mildly bawdy ditty that everyone misunderstands. Stiggins comes in drunk as a lord, and fat old Tony Weller dances around Stiggins while pummeling him. It seems as if valentines can lead to the bizarre marital difficulties of middle age, at least in Dickens' imagination. Perhaps Dickens uses a sugary tone in depicting young love to balance the souring comedy of marriage.

CHAPTER 34

Summary

Snodgrass and Mr. Perker hope that the jurymen have had a good breakfast, which means that they would be more likely to decide in favor of the defendant. At Guildhall, where the trial takes place, the Pickwickians, the lawyers, the spectators and the plaintiff are seated. Mrs. Bardell and her companions put on a little charade of misery. Mr.

Justice Stareleigh, the judge, a small, fat, stupid, testy man, concerns himself with irrelevancies. And after a reluctant juror is sworn in the trial begins.

Serjeant Buzfuz, the prosecuting attorney, tells of Mrs. Bardell's trusting innocence and Mr. Pickwick's villainy. He places a suspicious interpretation on Pickwick's casual notes to his landlady. Witnesses are called. Mrs. Cluppins eavesdropped on the conversation in which Mr. Pickwick "proposed." Winkle, who is badgered into confusion by the prosecution, adds further damaging evidence. Snodgrass and Tupman fare little better. Mrs. Sanders tells of circumstantial rumors. Finally Sam Weller cheerfully testifies that he knew nothing of the proposal, but he adds that Dodson and Fogg took the case on speculation, hoping to get money out of Pickwick. The case is summed up, and the jury finds Mr. Pickwick guilty, setting the damages at 750 pounds. On leaving, Mr. Pickwick says flatly that he would rather go to debtors' prison than pay.

Commentary

The trial is one of the most marvelous comic set-pieces in English literature. This is because Dickens understands the essential nature of a trial—it is a theater in which a contest takes place, a legal game with established rituals and rules. The game has nothing to do with justice or morality, except in a remote way; but it has everything to do with showmanship. In this struggle Mr. Pickwick's lawyers are hopelessly outclassed: Serjeant Snubbin has no life to him and Mr. Phunky is a nervous incompetent. Serjeant Buzfuz, for all the patent absurdity of his allegations, has a sound grasp of the nature and purpose of rhetoric, and his assistant thoroughly understands the tactics of cross-examination. They are playing for an audience, the jury, which will decide the winner. And they have a further advantage in that Mr. Pickwick's lawyers are on the defensive.

The only thing in Mr. Pickwick's favor is the testimony of Sam Weller, whose self-possession allows him to deflate the prosecution's case with one lethal remark about Dodson and Fogg. Possibly it is this remark that causes the jury to cut the damages in half, but even so Dodson and Fogg seem happy with the trial's outcome.

Dickens uses small details to good effect. Serjeant Buzfuz makes a big issue of Tommy Bardell's marbles, items that have no bearing on the case whatever but are used, fatuously, to establish a homely sympathy for Mrs. Bardell and her brat. Comedy is also present in Buzfuz's erotic interpretation of Mr. Pickwick's menu. Buzfuz's rhetoric, in fact, is a literary burlesque of courtroom procedure. Dickens' verve in carrying it to extremes of absurdity makes it successful.

In this chapter the time scheme is cleared up. It turns out that the Pickwickians began their travels the year before, in 1830, and that Mr. Pickwick "proposed" in July. This means that barely a month had elapsed before Mrs. Bardell started the lawsuit against him, surely a hasty decision on her part. With this new perspective, we can see that Dickens had forgotten his original date for the beginning of the travels, May 13, 1827. However, this perspective reinforces our sense of time in reading the novel as a series of successive adventures. But Dickens still telescopes time for his own purposes.

CHAPTERS 35-37

Summary

Mr. Pickwick remains adamant in his refusal to pay damages. On learning that it will be two months before he can be imprisoned, he decides to take his companions to Bath. He is accompanied by the Dowlers and listens to Captain Dowler advertise his own ferocity. At Bath the Pickwickians meet Angelo Cyrus Bantam, the master of ceremonies at a hotel. Bantam invites them to a ball, and Mr. Pickwick sends Sam for the tickets. Sam meets Bantam's snobbish footman and has some fun at his expense. The ball is fashionable and trivial, full of small talk, scandal, matchmaking, toadying, silliness, and glamour. Mr. Pickwick gets into a game of cards with three sharp, impatient socialites who intimidate him. He loses at cards and goes home to bed.

Since Mr. Pickwick and his friends plan to stay two months in Bath, they take private lodgings, which they share with the Dowlers. Life quickly settles into a pleasant routine centered on drinking mineral water. One evening Mr. Pickwick stays up to read "The True Legend of Prince Bladud," founder of Bath. One legend states that Bladud was cured of leprosy by the water of Bath. But the true story is that his father, the king, contracted a political marriage for him, while he had fallen in love with an Athenian lady. His father imprisons him, but Bladud escapes and flees to Athens, where he learns his sweetheart has married another. He ends up at Bath, where he wishes to die and is swallowed up by the earth. His tears are the source of the water of Bath.

Mr. Dowler falls asleep while waiting up for his wife, and she returns home very late. The door is locked, so the coachman sets up a heavy pounding that awakens Winkle, who comes to the door in his dressing gown and gets locked out. In embarrassment he tries to hide in Mrs. Dowler's sedan. Dowler awakes, thinking someone is trying to run off with his wife, and chases Winkle with a knife. Winkle escapes and prepares to leave at dawn, terrified by Dowler's threats.

Sam Weller is invited to a footman's "swarry" (soiree) by Bantam's footman, John Smauker. There is mutton and plenty to drink. The footmen all have a high sense of their own dignity, with which Sam has some good-humored fun. Each puts on airs but their low breeding keeps showing through. Sam, who is perfectly at ease, becomes the life of the party. The "swarry" ends in the morning hours with the footmen barely able to stagger home. The next day Mr. Pickwick tells Sam that Winkle has run off and sends him to find out where he went. Sam learns that Winkle went to Bristol. Mr. Pickwick then tells Sam to use any means to bring him back.

Commentary

The fertility of Dickens' imagination seems endless. In these chapters he introduces us to more than a dozen new and distinct characters, yet each bears some thematic relationship to what has gone before. Dowler, for example, recalls Peter Magnus, another coach companion of Mr. Pickwick's. While Dowler is harsh and supposedly fierce, and Magnus is nervous and effete, they both get violently jealous and threaten duels when a Pickwickian appears to be involved with their women. Winkle himself seems destined to get caught up in these misunderstandings.

The ball at Bath recalls the ball at Rochester, except that this is fancier, more crowded with socialites. Dickens takes a satirical attitude toward the foolishness, empty conceit, bootlicking, matchmaking, and nastiness of high society. Over all of this presides Angelo Cyrus Bantam, a dapper, effusive, illiterate, snobbish, silly fellow, as the master of ceremonies.

As an author Dickens himself is very much like a master of ceremonies, introducing the reader to hundreds of characters, telling an endless succession of anecdotes, and seeing that the reader has a good time. Dickens' virtue is that he sees through pomposity, cruelty, hypocrisy, selfishness, and conceit, which is something that Bantam cannot do.

The footman's "swarry" gives us a worm's eye view of high society. In Chapter 35 Dickens looks down on it from a superior moral position; here he shows us how it looks from below, through the eyes of the brightly uniformed footmen, who aspire to social dignity. Again, the servants ape the masters. The footmen wrap themselves in a spurious prestige that derives from their uniforms, just as their employers wrap themselves in a spurious dignity that stems from wealth and position. Dickens uses Sam Weller as the measure of the footmen and their values. Sam feels at ease anywhere because of his democratic belief in his own intrinsic worth. He does not have to put on airs: he knows he can cope with any situation just as he is.

The legends of Prince Bladud are a light piece of nonsense that mimics public relations material for Bath. Nevertheless, it takes up two recurrent themes in the novel, that of father-son relationships and the question of a mercenary or a disinterested marriage. Beyond this, it mirrors the action which follows. As Bladud runs from a political marriage, Winkle flees because of trouble over a woman. And Mr. Pickwick unexpectedly becomes like Bladud's harsh father when he sends Sam to bring back Winkle by any means.

CHAPTERS 38-39

Summary

At Bristol Winkle looks for directions and goes into a physician's shop, where he finds Bob Sawyer and Ben Allen. Sawyer tells Winkle the tricks he uses to get business, although he has no wares and few patients. Over brandy Ben Allen tells Winkle that Arabella is in the area, where she has been hidden to protect her from an unknown suitor. Ben wants his sister to marry Bob Sawyer. The news disturbs Winkle, who loves Arabella.

Winkle goes back to the hotel, where he meets Dowler, who is afraid that Winkle has followed him to Bristol to get even. Winkle, too, is frightened, but when he realizes what has happened he gets up his courage and magnanimously forgives Dowler. In bed that night Winkle is awakened by Sam Weller, who angrily accuses Winkle of adding to Mr. Pickwick's anxieties. Winkle is humbled but asks permission to stay until he can see Arabella. The next morning Sam sends word to Mr. Pickwick of the situation, having locked Winkle up for the night.

Mr. Pickwick arrives in Bristol to find out if Winkle's intentions toward Arabella are honorable. Winkle fervently declares they are, so

Mr. Pickwick sends Sam to locate Arabella. After hours of fruitless searching Sam accidentally finds his sweetheart Mary. Much kissing ensues, and Mary tells Sam that Arabella lives next door. Sam sees Arabella and tells her of Winkle's passionate love for her. After some hesitation she tells Sam that Winkle can see her the following night. With Mr. Pickwick to chaperon and Sam to guide him, Winkle has an interview with Arabella in which he learns that she loves him. Mr. Pickwick carries a powerful lantern, and the beam attracts the notice of a scientific gentleman, who writes a paper on the "atmospheric" phenomenon.

Commentary

These two chapters advance Winkle's romance with Arabella Allen and finish the business with Dowler. Dowler, of course, was a humbug from the start, and here his posturing is exposed. Winkle may be timorous and impulsive, too, but we sympathize with him because he never pretended to be brave. The duel with Slammer at Rochester cured him of any impulse to feign courage when he had nothing to gain.

As a suitor for Arabella's hand Winkle is by far the most presentable candidate. He may not have many virtues, but he is free of vices. Bob Sawyer, however, is disreputable, dissipated, unkempt, vulgar, boisterous, and irresponsible. One of Bob's reasons for wanting to marry Arabella is to get his hands on her money. Moreover, it is hard to imagine a fellow as independent as Sawyer scrambling over a garden wall to propose, as Winkle does.

Nevertheless, the reader enjoys Bob Sawyer as he can never enjoy Winkle. For all his boyish faults there is something admirable about Sawyer. His appeal lies in his good humor and carefree attitude in circumstances that would make anyone else crumble. His devices for getting patients when he has nothing to sell them are wonderfully quixotic. His friend, Ben Allen, on the other hand, is a dunce with no redeeming features. In his dissolution, he cannot hold his liquor without getting maudlin and pugnacious.

Sam Weller's loyalty to Mr. Pickwick is amply demonstrated in his reproachful treatment of Winkle. Sam realizes how much a man of principle his master is; and Winkle's flight to Bristol is an unworthy act to Sam, a desertion of Mr. Pickwick. Sam also points up another trait of Mr. Pickwick's, his youthfulness, on the expedition to see Arabella. Ordinarily strong principles and a boyish heart do not go together in an old man, but Dickens' achievement in creating Mr. Pickwick is to make us believe in him fully—and to make us love him.

The "scientific gentleman" is a measure of how much progress Dickens has made in characterizing Mr. Pickwick. At the beginning of this novel Dickens made his hero the butt of a joke very similar to this one: the inscription at Cobham in Chapter 11. To do this now would wreck our belief in Mr. Pickwick as a character. He has become much more human and sympathetic, a figure of comedy rather than farce. So Dickens creates the "scientific gentleman" as an object of farce. The gentleman, who has been waiting to make some unique discovery, finds it in Mr. Pickwick's lantern flashes. Like a good scientist, he investigates the hypothesis of his servant, who thinks it is burglars, and gets knocked on the head by Sam. In no way deterred, he writes a paper on the light flashes that makes him famous. Like Mr. Pickwick, this character exemplifies the resilience of human nature, but on a much lower level.

Many coincidences crop up in this section. Winkle asks for directions in Bristol and finds Bob Sawyer and Ben Allen. Dowler also flees to Bristol. Sam finds his sweetheart Mary in Bristol, living next door to Arabella Allen no less, hundreds of miles from where we last saw either girl. Dickens simply uses coincidence here to tie up loose plot ends before Mr. Pickwick goes to prison.

CHAPTERS 40-41

Summary

When his two-month stay in Bath is finished Mr. Pickwick returns to London. Three days later he is taken into custody by a rough, ostentatious sheriff's officer and his helper. Sam Weller puts up a fight but is restrained by Mr. Pickwick. At the sheriff's office Pickwick observes two young dissolutes. Mr. Perker arrives and attempts to dissuade Mr. Pickwick from going to prison but is unsuccessful. Perker then tells him they must wait for a writ of habeas corpus, which they obtain later that day. Mr. Pickwick and Sam are taken to the Fleet Prison for debtors. There Pickwick has to undergo the humiliation of "sitting for his portrait," which means allowing all of the turnkeys to scrutinize him closely. Mr. Pickwick sees about getting a bed for the night and is at last incarcerated in prison.

The warder, Tom Roker, leads Mr. Pickwick through foul, dingy passageways to his room, insisting upon the excellence of the accommodations. Sam Weller observes that prison does not harm idlers but it wrecks honest men, and he tells of a mild, anonymous prisoner who became so habituated to prison that freedom terrified him. Mr. Pickwick sends Sam to fetch his belongings and goes to bed for the night. He is awakened by his intoxicated roommates, who are exceptionally boisterous. One fellow snatches off Mr. Pickwick's nightcap and puts it on a companion's head, for which Pickwick jumps up and punches him. Another disagreeable roommate, Smangle, suggests they all have a drink at Pickwick's expense. Mr. Pickwick agrees, and Smangle cadges some cigars as well. While Mr. Pickwick tries to sleep Smangle boasts of his prowess for hours.

Commentary

Mr. Pickwick has a choice: he can pay Mrs. Bardell's damages or go to jail. Neither alternative is pleasant. If he paid up he would be rewarding three mercenary people, Mrs. Bardell and Dodson and Fogg. It would imply that they were right and he was wrong. If he goes to prison the law still triumphs. It can inflict a permanently miserable life on him. But Mr. Pickwick chooses prison, presumably because he himself would rather suffer than abet wrong by paying up. And although there may be principle behind the decision, it is backed up by strong elements of stubbornness and pique.

Here Mr. Pickwick starts to learn the consequences of his principles. He is finding out just how formidable the law can be. A new step is taking place in his education: he is learning that scoundrels like Dodson and Fogg have the power to subject him to misery for the rest of his life. There is no question of good triumphing, as it did when Jingle was exposed. Mr. Pickwick is beginning to see that evil can win indefinitely, but he refuses to give in to it no matter what the cost.

These chapters show Mr. Pickwick's arrest and his initiation into prison, which are highly unpleasant. The air of comedy is almost entirely muted. Dickens emphasizes the filth, the shabbiness, the sadness, and the squalor of the people and their surroundings. When the mood of a novel begins to change it is a good idea to pay attention to the diction and tone of the descriptive passages. When Mr. Pickwick is led to his room, for example, adjectives like "dirty," "dark," "narrow" recur frequently and convey the claustrophobic, grave-like, airless prison setting. The diction can convey a mood, just as musical notes convey a melody.

In addition, the characters we meet are very unsavory. The sheriff's officer and his aide seem like refugees from a penal colony. The young men in the sheriff's office are callous and despicable. The lame, ragged "bail" who accosts Mr. Pickwick is pitiable. The turnkeys are grim. Tom Roker extorts a good deal of money for cells and furnishings. Mivins, whom Pickwick hits, and Smangle are idle predators who thrive in prison. The human degradation of these chapters is sinister. Mr. Pickwick begins by thinking he can bear imprisonment with equanimity, but he soon realizes he is in a jungle of poverty, filth, misery, and rascality.

The difference between prison and freedom can be measured in two men: Smangle and Bob Sawyer. Both seem to flourish in conditions that would demoralize another person; both are dissipated and improvident; neither is above marrying for money. But Sawyer is a comic figure, while Smangle is distasteful. The difference lies mainly in their attitude toward Mr. Pickwick. Sawyer looks upon Pickwick as a boon companion, and Smangle sees him as a gullible person to be cheated. The scarcity of prison life determines Smangle's outlook, while the relative plenty available in the outside world determines Bob Sawyer's (even though Sawyer is quite poor).

CHAPTERS 42-45

Summary

Sam arrives with Mr. Pickwick's wardrobe the next morning and is about to come to blows with Smangle, when Smangle sees the clothes and craftily tries to obtain some. Determined to change rooms, Mr. Pickwick goes to see Tom Roker, who assigns him to a room with three dirty, sloppy ruffians. Mr. Pickwick learns from these three men that he can have a room to himself if he has the money. So he goes back to Roker and sublets a room from an embittered Chancery prisoner whose money has been drained off by the law courts. Having leased the cell, Mr. Pickwick goes to the poor prisoners' section to see about getting a man to run errands. There, among other specimens of dire misery, he encounters Alfred Jingle and Job Trotter. In extreme poverty they are shadows of their former selves. Mr. Pickwick is touched by their want and gives his former enemies some money. Returning to his room, Mr. Pickwick finds Sam waiting for him. Thinking that prison was no place for a young man, Mr. Pickwick tries to dismiss Sam but to continue his wages. While Sam disapproves of Mr. Pickwick's decision to go to prison, he refuses to hear of being dismissed and leaves quickly.

At the Insolvent Court Tony Weller and his companions stop by to see an old friend tried. Tony converses with a seedy, self-advertising lawyer named Sol Pell. While jostling for position in the courtroom, Tony comes upon his son, Sam. Sam informs him that his wife is showing the effects of too much liquor. Tony replies that Stiggins is suffering the same complaint. Sam also tells him of Mr. Pickwick's decision to dismiss him. Both men think that Mr. Pickwick will be plucked clean unless Sam assists him. So Sam borrows 25 pounds from his father and gets Tony to file suit against him in order to be jailed for debt with Mr. Pickwick. Solomon Pell handles the case. And Sam goes off to prison, celebrating along the way with Tony and his friends. Then Sam confronts Mr. Pickwick with the news that he, too, has been imprisoned for debt.

Mr. Pickwick insists on learning who Sam's creditor is, but Sam refuses to tell and diverts him with a long, absurd anecdote about a man who destroyed himself on principle. Sam is given a room with a good-humored cobbler, who tells how he was imprisoned because of legal squabbles over an inheritance. Smangle goes to Mr. Pickwick's room soon after this, announces that three friends have come to visit, and obtains money. Tupman, Snodgrass, and Winkle enter the room in a sad mood. Winkle has something on his mind which is agitating him. The Pickwickians enjoy a substantial meal with several bottles of wine. As Tupman and Snodgrass prepare to leave, Winkle tries to say something to Mr. Pickwick but cannot get the words out. Sam, however, asks a favor of Winkle, fully aware of what Winkle is up to. Later Tom Roker, the warder, announces to Mr. Pickwick that the Chancery prisoner from whom he obtained the room is about to die. Pickwick goes to see the man and finds him, in his dying moments, hoping that the Lord will remember his suffering.

In a few days Tony Weller brings his wife and Reverend Stiggins to see Sam. Tony is very mirthful, having shaken Stiggins up considerably during the coach ride. Stiggins and Mrs. Weller settle down to an afternoon of heavy drinking, as they moralize on Sam's condition. On leaving, Tony whispers to Sam that he has a plan for smuggling Mr. Pickwick out in a piano and shipping him to America. Sam finds Mr. Pickwick with Jingle and Job Trotter and is surprised to find them in such a wretched state. While Mr. Pickwick proposes something to Jingle, Sam treats Job Trotter to drink, over which Job expresses his admiration for Mr. Pickwick.

Later, in the prison yard, Mr. Pickwick becomes very distressed by the repetitive spectacle of misery, noise, dirt, squalor, and roughness of prison life. He decides to keep to his room, except for evening walks.

And he keeps to this resolution for three months, while his friends try to persuade him to pay the damages.

Commentary

The stagnation of prison is conveyed in a number of ways. Dickens tells us plainly at the end of Chapter 45 that the prisoners and the scenes are dreary repetitions of one another. Another indication is that people repeat the statements they have just made, presumably for emphasis, but the effect suggests a sort of mental vegetation. Finally, when Stiggins and Susan Weller visit Sam in prison they perform their act like windup dolls, moralizing and drinking. It is as if prison has cast a spell of stagnation on these two, and one can sense that Dickens no longer enjoys parading them about. The next we hear of them, Susan Weller has died and Stiggins gets his final comeuppance. In any case, the very state of being locked up is conducive to stagnation. After Mr. Pickwick makes his decision to avoid further contact with prison life, Dickens lets three months go by in one sentence so that he can pass on to the business of getting Mr. Pickwick out of prison.

The main emphasis of these chapters lies in how terrible a debtors' prison is, but Dickens conveys this with considerable verve. Dickens' success here lies in the multifaceted way he creates the prison atmosphere. Mr. Pickwick sees it as a pageant of degradation and filth. Sam and Tony Weller see it as a place that will cheat Mr. Pickwick of his eyeteeth. The Chancery prisoner sees it as a living grave. Susan Weller and Reverend Stiggins view it as the end of the road of bad morals. Smangle feels perfectly at home there. And Tom Roker views it as the whole of life, an earthly paradise in which he obtains preposterous sums from the prisoners for subhuman accommodations. Dickens' own opinion is also evident: a debtors' prison is a thoroughly unwholesome institution that ought to be abolished.

The effect of prison is startlingly evident in Alfred Jingle and Job Trotter. Physically thin to begin with, they have become positively emaciated. And more important, they have lost their vitality, impudence, and cunning—everything that mattered. The pair seem like deflated balloons, lacking the buoyance and mobility which was part of their essence. Hunger has robbed them of any urge to deceive. Indeed, in the poor prisoners' ward there is no point to deception, since everyone is in the same boat.

Once again Jingle's path crosses Mr. Pickwick's. Although Mr. Pickwick managed to expose Jingle at Ipswich, he made no impact whatever on Jingle's spirit. His triumph there was merely a matter of circumstance. But prison, in depriving Jingle of his impostures, prepares him for conversion. Prison becomes a test of morality, and Jingle's way of life cannot stand up to it. This development may be plausible, but the reader tends to resent it. For all his rascality Jingle was a source of delight. To make him vulnerable to morality is a sad disappointment.

Nevertheless, Dickens uses Jingle to show another development in Mr. Pickwick's education and character. In a world where one can be subjected to suffering for the rest of one's life, as the law can do to Mr. Pickwick, a man is at a dead end unless he can learn to forgive and show mercy. Jingle, of course, is the perfect recipient for Mr. Pickwick's forgiveness and compassion, since he had been Mr. Pickwick's nemesis for so long. However, Jingle had to be prepared to receive mercy, and the only way Dickens could do this was by deflating him, by depriving him of his old ebullience. Dickens was faced with a dilemma. He could use Jingle to show Mr. Pickwick's power of forgiveness, which the plot demanded; but to do so he would have to change Jingle's character completely. The solution may not be very satisfactory, yet under the circumstances Dickens did the best he could.

The basis of a debtors' prison was debt. Ironically, the prisoners have to pay for everything they get, for rooms, food, clothes, for errands they want performed. They even have to pay to keep unwanted roommates from living with them. For the first time Dickens calls attention to the power of money. Previously in the novel we had taken money for granted: the Pickwickians had enough to lead a leisurely life. But from now on Dickens will not allow us to forget money. In prison Mr. Pickwick comes up against a hard fact, the humiliation of not having enough money. From this premise stems all the shabbiness, the filth, the graft, the sadness of the place. Mr. Pickwick can afford to detach himself from prison life, because he has money. He can afford to view the Fleet as a pageant of distasteful or heartbreaking scenes, because his money protects him. If prison depresses him very much, he still does not succumb to the squalor. One wonders how prison would affect him if he were suddenly penniless.

Just as one learns the value of money in prison, one also learns the value of friendship. At one extreme is the Chancery prisoner, whose bitterest complaint is that prison has placed him beyond friendship. He is an exile from the human community and so prison is like a living grave to him. At the other extreme is Mr. Pickwick, who befriends everyone, including Smangle. Mr. Pickwick is not just a superficial friend, however. His relationship with Sam is deep. He is perfectly ready to sacrifice his own welfare to see that Sam lives in a wholesome environment, and even though he tries to dismiss Sam he intends to pay Sam's wages. Further, after Sam has himself jailed for debt in order to serve Mr. Pickwick, he wants to pay off Sam's creditor. This kind of mutual loyalty is the epitome of friendship, and Dickens makes it believable. Friendship is one of the supreme values for Dickens. It gives a man dignity and transcends all the misery of prison. Above all, it cannot be purchased, which gives it a greater power than money. It is in his immense capacity for friendship that the reader comes to love Mr. Pickwick.

In Chapter 42 Dickens speaks of Mr. Pickwick as "our excellent old friend," implying that his character is an actual person with whom he and the reader have established a kind of friendship. In a sense, by following Mr. Pickwick's adventures and coming to love him, we have gained an honorary membership in the Pickwick Club.

Dickens' technique of characterization is relevant here. He presents his characters as we would normally experience them in life — through their appearance, gestures, and speech. We can picture them vividly. And after they have made several appearances and we have become involved in their various adventures, we tend to regard them as we would old friends. Even the obnoxious characters come to seem rather like disagreeable acquaintances.

If Mr. Pickwick has been growing, so has Sam Weller. Sam disapproves of Mr. Pickwick's decision to remain in prison, but he has himself imprisoned to serve Mr. Pickwick. Moreover, he behaves generously to Job Trotter, not because his master has already done so but because he has absorbed Mr. Pickwick's principle of mercy. Sam's development is a reflection of Mr. Pickwick's. And as Sam's relationship to his master deepens, so does his affection for his father, Tony. Sam has become involved in his father's domestic woes, and the two men see each other frequently now.

Tony Weller tells Solomon Pell that Sam is "a reg'lar prodigy son!" Pell corrects him, "Prodigal, prodigal son, sir." And Tony replies huffily, "Never mind, sir. . . . I know wot's o'clock, sir. Wen I don't, I'll ask you, sir." Tony is perfectly right; Sam is a prodigy son, both to him and to Mr. Pickwick. Tony has a penchant for seemingly incorrect words that are poetically accurate.

70

CHAPTERS 46-47

Summary

The vixenish Mrs. Raddle, her browbeaten husband, and Mrs. Cluppins arrive at Mrs. Bardell's to go for an outing. Mrs. Bardell and her son and her group of friends take the coach to Hampstead, where they take tea. And poor Mr. Raddle is badgered all the way. As they dine, Mr. Jackson of Dodson and Fogg's comes to take Mrs. Bardell back to the city. She, her son, and two friends accompany him back, each ignorant of Mr. Jackson's purpose. He intimates that it has to do with a *cognovit* that Mrs. Bardell signed after the trial. Much to Mrs. Bardell's humiliation, she is imprisoned in Fleet Prison, where Mr. Pickwick is taking his evening walk. On seeing the woman, Sam Weller has a bright idea and sends Job Trotter to fetch Mr. Perker, the lawyer.

Mr. Perker arrives at the Fleet the next morning and proceeds to argue with Mr. Pickwick about why he should pay. Prison is no place for a woman, and Mrs. Bardell has agreed to forgo damages if Mr. Pickwick will pay her lawyers' fee. In addition, she has signed a paper saying that Dodson and Fogg egged her on. Besides this, Sam will remain in prison as long as Mr. Pickwick does. So if he chooses not to pay, public opinion will regard his obstinacy as reprehensible. Having set this forth, Mr. Perker is interrupted by Winkle and his new bride, Arabella. After congratulations, the pair ask Mr. Pickwick to break the news to her brother, Ben Allen, and his father, Mr. Winkle. The newlyweds think that Mr. Pickwick can reconcile these relatives to the marriage.

Mr. Pickwick relents and obtains his release and Mrs. Bardell's. He also agrees to see the Winkles' relatives. Sam then obtains his own release, and after a day of celebration Sam and Mr. Pickwick leave the Fleet the next morning.

Commentary

Mrs. Raddle, who was Bob Sawyer's landlady, appears as Mrs. Bardell's friend in this section. While these two landladies are widely different in temperament, neither of them hesitates to take advantage of a man. Mrs. Raddle uses fainting, nagging, and hysterics to reduce her husband to a state of quaking submission, while Mrs. Bardell uses a lawsuit in the hope of bringing Mr. Pickwick around. We are reminded that Mr. Pickwick is in prison because of Mrs. Bardell.

Mrs. Raddle is the nastiest woman in the novel. Not only does she aggressively strip her husband of his manhood, she allows her friends to do it as well. The point of the visit to Hampstead is that an innocent, peripheral member of the party, Mr. Raddle, is really the center of attention. He is under attack by almost every woman present. It is as if the women are getting even with him because Mr. Pickwick refuses to pay the damages.

The reader gets some humorous satisfaction from the reversal to which Mr. Jackson submits Mrs. Bardell in the company of her friends. He delivers them to the Fleet with all the polite, oily delicacy of a man who wants to avoid a scene. Mrs. Bardell receives a triple measure of poetic justice here. She is sent to prison by the same shysters she used against Mr. Pickwick. She is sent to the very same place. And she must confront the man she has wronged as she enters. We tend to rejoice in her dismay. However, in the very next chapter we are made to feel sorry for her. As Mr. Perker points out, prison will degrade her. She has no way of getting out unless Mr. Pickwick pays her legal fees. Poetic justice comes up against the harsh reality of Fleet Prison and is instantly shown to be no justice at all, unless Mr. Pickwick is willing to show Mrs. Bardell mercy. The way Dickens manipulates this double perspective of poetic justice and the actuality of prison is masterly. The real justice of Mrs. Bardell's situation is that she is now placed at Mr. Pickwick's mercy.

Dickens also shows a double perspective in Mr. Perker's attitudes. From a professional point of view Perker admires the way Dodson and Fogg got Mrs. Bardell to sign a *cognovit*. But he quickly sees how her imprisonment can be used to get Mr. Pickwick and her out of the Fleet. The law may have corrupted his intellect but it has made no impression on his heart, which is ready to work for good. The law can be a road to perdition, but a decent man like Perker survives the temptations.

Mr. Perker presents the sound, negative reasons for paying Dodson and Fogg: because of the suffering and misunderstanding that refusing to pay will cause. However, Winkle and Arabella present a positive, romantic reason for paying: Mr. Pickwick is the only person they can trust to reconcile their relatives to the marriage. The reader fully expected that Winkle would elope with Arabella, but that this marriage should partly effect Mr. Pickwick's release is unexpected. As a result, the reader tends to delight in the marriage, just as Perker and the Pickwickians do. Dickens practically makes us feel like a member of the party.

Having learned forgiveness and charity toward the people who have wronged him, and having plumbed the depths of friendship, it is entirely appropriate that Mr. Pickwick should undertake a mission in the service of true love.

Mr. Pickwick spends as much time in prison as Dickens' father spent when Dickens was twelve – that is, about three months. Dickens, of course, has been reworking that childhood calamity in his novel. Sam Weller is Dickens as he would like to have been during that time: self-reliant, witty, cheerful, experienced, able to handle himself in any situation. And Mr. Pickwick is what Dickens wished his father could have been: protective, affluent, responsible, unselfish. Dickens idealized his relationship with his father in *Pickwick Papers*, but his mother reappears in many guises as the threatening middle-aged woman. Dickens never forgave his mother for wanting to send him back to the blacking factory after he had been taken out. While these psychological pressures are behind the novel, Dickens' writing ability alone transformed his fantasies into a towering art.

CHAPTERS 48-51

Summary

Bob Sawyer and Ben Allen are in their Bristol shop discussing their prospects. They have clients but very few can pay. The best thing would be for Bob to marry Arabella and use her 1,000 pounds, except that Arabella has no liking for Bob. As they talk of the revenge they would take on another suitor, Ben Allen's aunt enters to announce that Arabella has run off and gotten married. Ben Allen, suspecting his aunt's servant of being an accomplice, violently attacks him. Mr. Pickwick arrives with Sam and the fight is broken up. Then Mr. Pickwick tells the group that Arabella has married Nathaniel Winkle. Suspicions and angry words follow, but things settle down after Sawyer, Allen, and the rest take hearty gulps from a liquor bottle. Ben becomes partially reconciled to his sister's marriage and agrees to go with Mr. Pickwick to see Winkle's father, who lives in Birmingham. Mr. Pickwick and Sam retire to their inn, where they catch the one-eyed bagman from Eatanswill about to tell the tale of the bagman's uncle.

The bagman's uncle, a hard-drinking cloth salesman, had consumed a great deal of liquor at a friend's home in Edinburgh. He was walking to his lodging when he came across a yard full of old, discarded mail coaches. He sat down on an old axletree and dozed off, but he awoke to find the coaches restored and ready to leave. Three other passengers arrive: a gentleman, a ruffian, and a lady imploring help. The ruffian assaults the bagman's uncle and is defeated temporarily. Their coach begins its journey and then stops at a deserted house, where the four passengers alight. In the house the lady's two abductors try to kill the bagman's uncle, but with her help both of them are slain. The lady informs the uncle that their lives are still in danger, so they mount the coach and dash off, pursued by the gentleman's henchmen. In the morning the bagman's uncle finds himself on the deserted coach.

The next morning Mr. Pickwick arrives at Sawyer's shop to get Ben Allen for the trip to Birmingham. Bob Sawyer closes his shop for good and, uninvited, he climbs up on the coach. Mr. Pickwick begins to notice that passersby keep staring at them and learns that Bob Sawyer is performing pranks on top of the coach. Sawyer offers Pickwick and Allen a flask of milk-punch, and before long Mr. Pickwick rather enjoys the pranks. But as the coach draws near Birmingham that evening Mr. Pickwick becomes apprehensive about Sawyer's presence. His fears are justified, for Sawyer continues to clown in the Winkle home while Ben Allen is sleepily drunk, which makes Mr. Pickwick's mission more precarious. Mr. Winkle sternly puts a damper on the antics. After reading a long letter from his son that tells of the marriage, Mr. Winkle curtly tells Mr. Pickwick that he will think the matter over and decide what to do later, adding that he is greatly disappointed in his son's companions. Angry and worried, Mr. Pickwick leaves, taking Sawyer and Allen with him.

The depressed group gets a late start for London the next day and is caught in a continuous heavy downpour. After traveling some hours they decide to stay the night at an inn in Towcester. Mr. Pickwick gets a note off to Winkle telling of his arrival in London the following day. Sam Weller finds Pott, the windbag editor of the *Eatanswill Gazette,* who is also staying there. Sam invites him to join Mr. Pickwick, which he does. Pott says he intends to go to a ball given by the opposition party. Mrs. Pott has left him and taken half his property, and Pott is vengefully happy to hear that Winkle has married. Mr. Slurk, the editor of the *Eatanswill Independent* and Pott's mortal enemy, also stops at that inn on his way to the ball. Bob Sawyer, sensing an opportunity for mischief, leads Pott into Slurk's company, where insults lead to blows. Mr. Pickwick attempts to separate the two men and gets banged up. The battle ends when Sam subdues Pott and has Slurk disarmed. Then everyone goes to bed, and next morning they leave for London.

Commentary

The most prominent character in these chapters, aside from Mr. Pickwick, is Bob Sawyer. His pranks may lead to embarrassments and fighting, but they enliven the narrative considerably. Bob Sawyer is the perennial life of the party here, a boisterous practical joker who seizes any opportunity for fun. His exuberant clowning serves to cast off the shadow of prison, to help restore Mr. Pickwick to the vital, active world of freedom. Episodes involving Bob Sawyer seem to fall at crucial points in the story—prior to the trial, just before Mr. Pickwick is imprisoned and just after he is released. It is as if the unpleasantness of legal action and prison life requires some vigorous, life-enhancing buffoon to set it off and relieve it.

One important feature of these chapters is violent activity and fighting. After being pent-up, so to speak, in the dreariness of prison, the narrative now shows an explosion of animal spirits. When Mr. Pickwick and Sam walk into Sawyer's shop Ben Allen is trying to strangle his aunt's servant. In the bagman's tale about his uncle the fighting is lethal. Then Pott and Slurk attack each other with a satchel and a poker, thrashing Mr. Pickwick in the process. And while Sam tries to stop the fight Sawyer and Allen are dancing around the combatants, looking for wounds they can doctor.

Another feature of these chapters is the sensation of movement, since much of the action takes place in coaches. The bagman's uncle rides his ghost coach, and Mr. Pickwick and his companions ride from Bristol to Birmingham to Towcester. Travel itself is shown to be a pleasure, especially after the stagnation of prison. One of the delights of this novel is the vivid way it portrays the coaching days of England. Dickens himself loved to make journeys, and his joy in them is quite evident in this section. We get a sense of the comfort and pleasure to be had in wayside inns and hotels, the enjoyment a storyteller like the bagman could give, and how riding whetted one's appetite and thirst. We realize how important good companions were in traveling. All of these revelations suddenly come into focus after Mr. Pickwick has undergone the confinement of prison. The reader, too, feels liberated once the action is back on the coach roads.

A third emphasis in this portion falls on good food and copious drinking, which contrasts with the poor prison food and wine and ale. A sense of plenty is restored to the novel. Mr. Pickwick seems determined to make up for lost time, and Dickens indulges him to the full.

Three characters from Eatanswill turn up in this section: the bagman, Mr. Pott, and Mr. Slurk. Almost a year has passed since Pott and the bagman made their last appearance, and they seem like old acquaintances. Like the traditional traveling salesman, the bagman seems to specialize in stories about traveling salesmen. His tale about his uncle bears an indirect relationship to Winkle. Just as the uncle rescued the lovely woman from two villains, so Winkle rescued Arabella from the clutches of Ben Allen and Bob Sawyer. The dream adventure expresses the wish of many inconsequential men to lead a dashing life and win a beautiful woman. Winkle seems to live an adventurous life in spite of himself, and he has won an attractive young lady. Once again, the interpolated tale mirrors the action of the novel.

The fight between Pott and Slurk puts a comic end to the political satire in the novel. Even though Pott's wife has left him, Pott promised to thrash Slurk to uphold her honor after Slurk printed the poem suggesting that Winkle had cuckolded Pott. Pott was too much in love with his own voice to keep a wife happy. And here his editorial rhetoric has grown even flowery. Slurk is Pott's mirror-image, the double he wants to destroy. Each man seems bent on annihilating the other, a drive that is ultimately self-destructive. The situation is a comic version of Poe's story "William Wilson."

The plot of these chapters concerns Mr. Pickwick's mission to reconcile the relatives to Winkle's marriage. If he succeeds with Ben Allen, he is far from successful with Winkle's father. Mr. Winkle, Sr., apparently holds a different idea of parental responsibility than the childless Pickwick. While Mr. Pickwick goes to great lengths to assist young Winkle, Winkle's own father thinks the way to raise a son is to keep him in boarding schools and then send him out in the world with an unknown, elderly chaperon. Mr. Winkle seems like a brusque, stern, businesslike man, but as a father he is irresponsible. His remoteness from his son explains why young Winkle wrote him a letter and sent Mr. Pickwick to break the news. A further point is that it is important for Winkle to get his father's approval, since Mr. Winkle controls his son financially. Mr. Pickwick, on the other hand, exercises his fatherly authority over Winkle through affection. The interview between the two men would not have been satisfactory even if Sawyer and Allen had not been along, because there was little basis for a common understanding. Mr. Winkle seems interested in Arabella's dowry, while Mr. Pickwick is interested in the couple's happiness.

These chapters take place at the end of July, 1831, and show us three consecutive days of a five-day trip. The time scheme is quite clear, which reflects the specific purpose of the trip. Mr. Pickwick has a special aim and wastes no time in seeing that he fulfills it. In general, throughout the novel the adventures which involve some purpose on Mr. Pickwick's part have a tighter sense of time than those which do not.

CHAPTERS 52-54

Summary

Back in London Sam's sweetheart, Mary, who has become the Winkle's maid, tells Sam that there is a letter for him. After kissing and flirting with Mary, Sam reads that his stepmother has died and that Tony wants him to visit. Sam takes a leave of absence from Mr. Pickwick and goes to Dorking, where he finds his father in a melancholy state because of his wife's death. Sam learns that the Dorking spinsters and widows are already trying to catch Tony. Before her death Susan Weller repented of her attachment to the wrong kind of religion. She also left Sam 200 pounds to be invested in funds, and she left Tony the bulk of her estate. While Sam is visiting, the Reverend Stiggins enters to find out if Mrs. Weller bequeathed anything to him. As he helps himself to the rum, Tony Weller jumps up and starts kicking him violently into the street.

Mr. Pickwick tells Arabella of his unsuccessful encounter with Mr. Winkle. He comforts her by telling her that Mr. Winkle may change his mind in time, and that even if he doesn't Winkle will be helped by Mr. Pickwick.

Mr. Pickwick then goes to Mr. Perker's office to take care of a number of things. He has arranged for Jingle's and Job Trotter's release from prison and has gotten them positions in the West Indies. Jingle seems rather confused and abashed, but both men are appreciative. After they leave, Mr. Pickwick talks to Perker of the possibility of Mr. Winkle's relenting, and Mr. Perker tells him to leave that to Arabella, who could charm anyone. Finally, Dodson and Fogg arrive to be paid. They are self-assured and oily, obviously pleased at receiving the money. As they leave Mr. Pickwick calls them "a well-matched pair of mean, rascally, pettifogging robbers," shouting the words after them. Mr. Perker breaks out laughing; and Pickwick, relieved by the outburst, becomes placidly benevolent again. Then there is a furious knocking at the door.

It is Joe the Fat Boy, who announces Mr. Wardle. Wardle enters the office delighted to see his two friends. He says he has brought Emily to see her friend, Arabella, and that Emily is considering an elopement with Snodgrass. When he first heard of it he made a great fuss, but he is evidently more or less reconciled to their match despite his irascible manner. The men agree to have dinner together that evening, and Mr. Wardle sends Joe the Fat Boy back to the hotel to report these arrangements. Joe surprises Emily with Snodgrass and has to be bribed to keep quiet. Joe also becomes infatuated with Sam's sweetheart, Mary. Later that day Snodgrass retreats to the bedroom when he hears Wardle enter. The Wardles, Winkle and his wife, Ben Allen, and Mr. Pickwick assemble for dinner. Snodgrass sends the stupid Joe for help, but the fat boy succeeds only in arousing everyone's suspicion. Finally, Snodgrass makes an appearance – to Mr. Wardle's angry amazement and Mr. Pickwick's astonishment. However, Snodgrass declares his undying love and devotion to Emily; and when Wardle shows his gratification the gathering becomes happy and spirited.

Commentary

These chapters complete certain plot strands and prepare us for the end of the book. Susan Weller dies, providing Sam and Tony with a modest legacy. Reverend Stiggins gets his comic punishment from Tony Weller. Jingle and Job Trotter are packed off to the West Indies for moral rehabilitation. We are given the hope that Arabella may win over Winkle's father. Dodson and Fogg are paid 133 pounds and sent off with Mr. Pickwick's denunciation ringing in their ears. Lastly Mr. Wardle reappears, and Snodgrass' romance with Emily is approaching its destined conclusion at the altar. The many plots that Dickens has been juggling in the air are beginning to come to rest. Dickens deals out justice according to the time-honored method of the comic author. There are kicks or insults for the incorrigibly selfish. There is hope for the penitent rascals, who are sent away to begin a new life. There is freedom for the victimized husband. There is marriage for the worthy young lovers. And there is universal love and respect for the benevolent old hero.

Behind the happy ending there is an implicit belief in Providence, in a supernatural power that guides the affairs of men just as the author guides the destiny of his characters. The novel is a testing ground of morality in which the strongest eventually win out. From the way Dickens is beginning to end this novel we can see that there is a hierarchy of values, with Mr. Pickwick at the top and Dodson and Fogg at the bottom. The whole course of Mr. Pickwick's education has led to the affirmation of Christian charity and goodwill among men. These values, exemplified in Mr. Pickwick, are the strongest in the novel and place Mr. Pickwick at the center of the human community, where he radiates in all directions. Dodson and Fogg, who represent conniving selfishness, are banished to the fringes of the human community by Mr. Pickwick's excoriation, where they are promptly forgotten.

We have seen that Dickens cannot portray a serious romance with authority or conviction. The reason becomes plain in this section. It is not just the coy or maudlin tone that Dickens affects. Dickens basically has no sense of the nuances of courtship, of the delicate progressions and regressions that occur between couples. Sam's romance with Mary, for example, has remained on the same level from the first. It consists of flirtatious gestures, rudimentary conversation, and a lot of kissing. Further, Snodgrass and Emily are emblematic lovers: we see almost nothing of the way they court. Dickens' lovers merely repeat the same gestures and tokens over and over, and love seems like a mechanical process that leads to the altar. In actuality courtship brings out a person's creativity, and love can serve to reveal a person's essential nature. But in *Pickwick Papers* love reveals nothing about a character. It is simply a convenient fictional device.

Fortunately Dickens has a good sense of timing. He never dwells too long in areas where he is weak. As a result the novel moves swiftly and interestingly along right to the end. For one thing Dickens' power of invention never flags. Even as Sam flirts with Mary there is a wonderfully comic letter from Tony to engage the reader. One wonders how a wife's death can be humorous without being in bad taste, but Dickens manages it with finesse. Or consider the way Snodgrass' romance with Emily is handled. Both are the dullest of characters. Yet Dickens galvanizes Joe the Fat Boy into life and a series of scenes become charged with interest. Without Joe these scenes would be stale and tedious, and the impending marriage would seem perfunctory. This stupid, greedy, clumsy, infatuated fellow becomes for the time being one of the most fascinating persons in the world. Dickens' ability to dramatize such unlikely characters and make them serve the plot is little less than brilliant.

Even when conveying information through his characters, Dickens can make insipid facts dance with revelation. Mr. Perker's feckless clerk, Peter Lowten, informs Mr. Pickwick that Job Trotter has decided to go with Jingle to the West Indies rather than accept a more lucrative position with Mr. Perker. Lowten obviously thinks Job Trotter is a fool, showing himself to be a cynical and self-seeking young man. The law may have corrupted him, but he does not gain much from his corruption, being only a clerk.

If Dickens is poor at depicting romance, his sense of tone in depicting male friendships is infallible. The discussions between Sam and Tony Weller and between Mr. Wardle, Mr. Perker, and Mr. Pickwick are rich in nuance. The reader can feel the exact inflections of the talk. We know what each man is like. We know the pleasure each gets from friendship. And we, too, derive enjoyment from the direction and flavor of their conversations. There is nothing perverse about this. Most men get deep satisfaction from the ease and freedom they feel in the company of other men.

One regrets the transformation of Jingle from a light, amoral, vivacious figure of comedy to a depressed, spiritless, confused, melodramatic penitent. Dickens himself seems embarrassed by the change; as a stage manager he tries to make Jingle's last appearance as brief as possible. Dickens knew very well of course that he made Jingle an irresistible character. To change him, even to fulfill the plot, must have seemed like a dirty trick.

CHAPTERS 55-56

Summary

Tony Weller finds the will his wife made out, in which she gives 200 pounds to Sam and the rest to Tony. Sam tells his father that the will must be probated before they can come into their inheritance. So the two men go to see Solomon Pell, taking a group of coachmen along to umpire. The legal formalities take about a week, and the skinny Pell begins to put on weight from this new income. When the will has passed through probate Pell takes the men over to a stockbroker to invest Sam's 200 pounds. The broker, a gaudy fellow named Wilkins Flasher, Esq., is fond of making bets on every topic of conversation. He receives Sam's portion of the legacy, and Solomon Pell takes a large fee, which leaves Tony Weller with over 1,100 pounds. Mr. Weller decides to see Mr. Pickwick with the money.

After being ushered into Mr. Pickwick's room, Tony finds himself speechless. At length he manages to say that he intends Mr. Pickwick to have the money, places it in Mr. Pickwick's hands, and tries to escape, but Sam restrains him. Mr. Pickwick is reluctant to accept the money but decides he can use it to set Sam up in business, which would enable Sam to marry. However, Sam steadfastly refuses to leave Mr. Pickwick's service, saying that Mary will have to wait. Tony is very pleased by his son's loyalty to Mr. Pickwick.

Meanwhile an old gentleman enters looking for Arabella's room. He enters, intimates that he represents Winkle's father and charges Arabella with imprudence in marrying Nathaniel. She does not deny it, but tearfully defends herself, and the old man relents a bit. Then young Winkle enters, sees his father and defends both his wife and his decision. His father then shows himself to be very delighted with the match. Mr. Pickwick comes in and is gratified to see Mr. Winkle's change of heart.

Sam, on learning of Joe the Fat Boy's crush on Mary, gives him a ceremonious kick.

Commentary

These chapters show Tony Weller's innocence and goodwill, among other things. The only world in which he is at home is that of coaching. Widows and the law are two realities that threaten him, just as they threatened Mr. Pickwick. The former are rejected out of hand; the latter requires Sam's help. Having found his wife's will, his first impulse is to burn it up, assuming that he can take over his legacy immediately. So Sam has to take the matter in hand and guide his father through the mazes of legal and financial procedure. And having obtained the estate in cash, Tony rushes over to Mr. Pickwick's hotel and tries to hand the money over to Mr. Pickwick's care as quickly as possible. He has no conception of how to use it. Money is a burden to him because he wants to remain irresponsible and free of worry. His coachman's life is ideally suited to his character: when things become oppressive he has only to get up on a coach and ride off.

The irresponsible use of money is also revealed in Wilkins Flasher, the stockbroker, who in a minute or two makes three substantial bets on topics that arise in the course of conversation. It is as if he can only communicate with someone by making bets, which is like an impersonal challenge. One shudders to think how Sam's money is going to be invested. As a character Wilkins Flasher, Esq., is created through his speech: he is the quintessential speculator.

It is surprising how much of the action in these closing chapters revolves around money. We are concerned about Arabella's ability to placate old Mr. Winkle because he has the power to deprive his son of an income or a livelihood. And Mr. Pickwick has been considering setting both Winkle and Sam up in business with his own money.

Character determines the way one uses money, and in this section we see four different attitudes toward its use. Tony wants to get rid of it, because money draws widows. Wilkins Flasher uses it to speculate, to make it a way of relating to others. Mr. Winkle's tendency is to use it as a weapon to enforce compliance. And Mr. Pickwick wants to bestow it on worthy young men who have no way of establishing themselves. Mr. Pickwick again reveals his moral superiority in this. But as it turns out, none of his friends need or want help. Even Jingle has sworn to pay Mr. Pickwick back. However, the reader can easily picture Wilkins Flasher committing suicide as a bankrupt, especially after he bet on the suicide of a bankrupt. Here we see some of the ways in which superfluous money can be used, from a high moral level to a low moral level. And after the poverty of Fleet Prison all this ready money reminds us that the world of this novel is fundamentally an affluent one.

Though Sam must act like a father to Tony as he guides him through probate, Sam reaffirms his sonship to Mr. Pickwick when he postpones his marriage in order to continue serving the old man. An important sacrifice takes place here. Mr. Pickwick offers to set Sam up in business even though he knows he will be very lonely without Sam, but he wants to do this so that Sam can marry. Sam responds to this generosity by postponing his marriage. Each man recognizes his obligation to the other even when it is not in his own best interest. This mutual loyalty and Sam's sacrifice parallel what occurred in the Fleet, when Sam had himself jailed for debt to serve his master. Once again we are reminded of how deep their relationship goes.

In this first novel Dickens discovered a technique that he would use in novel after novel and develop to a high pitch of virtuosity—the device of using characters to explore many aspects of a central situation so that the characters bear a thematic relationship to one another. We have seen how the middle-aged women are comic predators. But the most important use of this technique has to do with father-son ties.

Pickwick Papers has three basic types of fathers: the genial, benevolent ones (Mr. Pickwick and Tony Weller); the ones with rough exteriors and soft hearts (Mr. Wardle and Mr. Winkle); and the savage fathers of the interpolated tales. This last group is excluded from the comic world of the narrative proper, and quite rightly. In the other types there is a subdivision. There is the responsible, benevolent fatherly type in Mr. Pickwick, who tries to aid and advise the young men in his protection. Then there is the irresponsible, benevolent father in Tony Weller, who let Sam run the streets from an early age without guidance. Of fathers who have a rough manner and a tender heart, Mr. Wardle is the responsible one. He cares about his sister and daughters and wants to see that they make good marriages. Mr. Winkle, on the other hand, has given his son little guidance, leaving his education to boarding schools and to Mr. Pickwick. Dickens, in effect, has presented a rather thorough picture of the various kinds of fathers that can inhabit a comic world. But his real achievement lies in the way he gives them life: they may be types, but each enjoys a special energy and will of his own.

CHAPTER 57

Summary

After a week of mysterious trips Mr. Pickwick announces to his friends that he is settling down for good in a newly purchased and furnished home at Dulwich. The Pickwick Club has disbanded. And he tells everyone that the wedding of Snodgrass and Emily Wardle will take place in his new home. Preparations are made, and the wedding is a glorious affair.

Nathaniel Winkle obtains a position in London from his father. Augustus Snodgrass settles down to being a country gentleman. Tracy Tupman takes rooms at Richmond, where he remains a bachelor. Bob Sawyer and Ben Allen go to India as surgeons, and after learning temperance they do well. Jingle and Job Trotter become useful members of society in the West Indies. Tony Weller retires a year later because of gout and lives upon the income from the money Mr. Pickwick invested for him. After two years Sam Weller weds Mary, and both of them serve Mr. Pickwick. And Mr. Pickwick himself becomes godfather to the many children of his friends, living on as a widely respected and much loved old man.

Commentary

Even though we anticipate the novel's ending, this final chapter comes as a shock. We are saddened to realize that the characters have given up their rollicking adventures to settle down for good. After the vitality, the joy, the grand celebrations, the odd vital characters who enlivened the novel, the prospect of this glorious, absurd world losing its energy at last is regrettable. Yet the various plots have been exhausted and we know all we need to know about the characters.

The last several paragraphs resemble a newsy letter from an old friend telling one how one's mutual acquaintances are doing. The assumption that Dickens' invented characters are actual persons that we might meet anywhere is encouraged throughout the book, and we do come to feel that they are like old friends.

Even though Dickens has related the novel in the past tense and writes the last paragraph in the present tense to suggest that Mr. Pickwick is still alive, we do not get a feeling of the novel's "pastness" until the last chapter. When Dickens uses the past tense in the preceding chapters he gives us a sense of immediacy through constant dialogue and dramatic exchange, through presenting the sights and sounds of his scenes. The reader feels as if he were witnessing the scenes as they happen. But here Dickens suddenly stops dramatizing the action and merely narrates it. The drama ends and we get something like a newsy letter from the author.

Nevertheless, Dickens has created a vision of what the world might be like, in Dingley Dell, if only we had the good will, the purpose and energy to make it so. He seems to feel that the Kingdom of God can be achieved, here and now, in our hearts. Fellowship, romance, adventure, innocence and youthfulness are perennial values, and Dickens gave them great and wonderful form in *Pickwick Papers*.

NOTES ON THE MAJOR CHARACTERS

SAMUEL PICKWICK

Mr. Pickwick is one of Dickens' greatest creations. A fat old man who becomes a romantic adventurer, Mr. Pickwick acquires form and character as the novel progresses. He has misadventures because he is living in a spiritual Eden, unaware of the presence of deception; then he undergoes a moral education. By the end of the novel he has become the incarnation of Christian charity and goodwill. His growth is entirely convincing, one of Dickens' very few instances of success in showing a believable, virtuous character.

A large part of Dickens' achievement in creating Mr. Pickwick lies in the three-dimensionality of the portrait. Dickens does not develop his characters the way a modern novelist does, by showing their internal conflicts. Dickens depicts his characters from the outside, through their speech, appearance, and gestures. Nevertheless, he gives us a full portrait of Mr. Pickwick's character, and the spiritual development can be inferred from the actions. Mr. Pickwick is loyal and protective toward his friends, gallant toward women, hot-tempered toward the nasty or unscrupulous, affectionate and self-sacrificing toward his servant, forgiving and merciful toward persons who have wronged him. He is also boyish, innocent, fun-loving, a bit absurd as he goes from one scrape to another.

The adventures have a definite pattern to them, which reveals Mr. Pickwick's character. One plot involves trying to frustrate Jingle's matrimonial schemes; another deals with fighting Mrs. Bardell's breach-of-promise suit; a third involves aiding true love. Each of these plot lines has to do with romance, with combating mercenary plans and furthering disinterested love. Even though Dickens cannot draw serious love successfully, we believe in Mr. Pickwick's efforts to assist it.

Finally, Dickens reveals Mr. Pickwick's character through his relationship to Sam Weller. Sam begins simply as Mr. Pickwick's valet. Then he becomes emotionally involved in his master's attempts to thwart Jingle and Mrs. Bardell, which establishes him as an ally. Then in prison both men prove their willingness to make personal sacrifices for the other, and Sam becomes like a son to Mr. Pickwick. It is partly in the growing depth of their relationship that we come to accept Mr. Pickwick as a real person.

SAM WELLER

As a character Sam Weller complements Mr. Pickwick, just as Sancho Panza complements Don Quixote. Whereas Mr. Pickwick is innocent and elderly, Sam is experienced and young, the most intelligent character in the novel. If Mr. Pickwick loses his temper easily, Sam is quite self-possessed. While Mr. Pickwick has no romantic intentions, Sam carries on a courtship through much of the novel. One really cannot discuss Sam Weller without reference to Mr. Pickwick.

This is partly functional, since Sam's life is thoroughly intertwined with his master's, as a servant, ally, and son-figure. But it is also spiritual. Dickens implies that Sam's practical knowledge should be in the service of Mr. Pickwick's Christian principles. In other words, Dickens shows in the relationship that a good head should serve a good heart. Mr. Pickwick gives Sam purpose, and Sam gives Mr. Pickwick the practical basis to effect the purpose. However, each is a unique and delightful personality in his own right.

TONY WELLER

Mr. Pickwick becomes like a father to Sam, but Tony Weller is Sam's actual father. He is generous, innocent, fat, and old like Mr. Pickwick, and both men are threatened in some way by widows and the law. Unlike Mr. Pickwick, Tony is wholly irresponsible as a father, a quality that his job as a coachman has helped to foster. Having let Sam run the streets at an early age, Tony has had no share in his son's upbringing. Tony is a poor husband as well, having let his wife take up with an unsavory evangelist.

However, Sam and Tony become quite close during the novel. Each feels affection for the other, and as Sam becomes closer to Mr. Pickwick, his relationship with his father also grows deeper. Despite the love Sam feels for Tony, he does not respect his father as an authority. The two men are more like warm friends.

MR. WARDLE

Like Tony Weller, Mr. Wardle can be compared to Mr. Pickwick. Wardle, too, is benevolent, hot-tempered, responsible, fat, and old; but he is also coarser and more aggressively masculine than Mr. Pickwick. He enjoys sports and hunting, which Mr. Pickwick indulges in only when he is present. He is also accustomed to giving orders, a thorough country squire.

As a character Mr. Wardle is overshadowed by his estate at Dingley Dell. Manor Farm is capacious, full of the good things of life. It has huge festive gatherings, plenty to eat and drink, storytelling, singing, recitation, dancing, sporting activities, card games, romance — something for everyone in fact. The place is conceived as a hospitable refuge from the knockabout world of the road and the chicanery of London. The reader enjoys this idyllic spot, where life unfolds slowly and naturally. At the beginning of the novel Trundle is courting Isabella Wardle; in the middle they are married; and by the end Isabella is pregnant. Dickens has created in the Wardle home a kind of earthly paradise.

ALFRED JINGLE

Jingle is one of the most engaging rascals in literature, a tall, thin, shabby young man with a gift for imposture and a hilarious staccato patter. Jingle is Mr. Pickwick's negative, an alter ego whose career parallels Mr. Pickwick's precisely. The two men meet as Pickwick starts out on his first adventure and from thenceforth their paths cross at regular intervals. Jingle teaches Mr. Pickwick the power and reality of deception, and three of Mr. Pickwick's adventures are concerned with frustrating Jingle's matrimonial plans. Jingle acquires a servant at the same time Mr. Pickwick hires Sam. And although Jingle and Job Trotter win out at Bury St. Edmunds, Mr. Pickwick and Sam triumph at Ipswich. Both pairs are sent to debtors' prison, where they are transformed. Mr. Pickwick learns forgiveness and Jingle learns humility. Finally, Jingle and his servant settle in the West Indies, while Mr. Pickwick and Sam settle at Dulwich. Mr. Pickwick's relationship to Jingle is something like that of a father to a prodigal son.

BOB SAWYER

Sawyer is something of a rowdy version of Alfred Jingle; a young man completely without parental guidance. He would like to marry Arabella Allen and have her money, but he also genuinely likes her. He is inventive, coming up with several ingenious, hapless tricks to increase his medical practice. Like Jingle, he is always hoping for easy money, enjoys practical jokes, and is quick to strike up acquaintances. Sawyer may be a failure — improvident, hard drinking, slovenly, boisterous, impulsive — but he enjoys life and the reader responds to his uncouth charm.

LITERARY DEVICES

COMEDY

The comedy of *Pickwick Papers* is more than the use of humorous techniques, although it includes these. Comedy is essentially an attitude toward the world, a way of selecting and viewing human behavior. The funniness of comedy lies as much in the author's point of view as it does in the actions he depicts.

One large element of Dickens' point of view is irreverence for certain established institutions. The law, the military, the medical, the evangelistic, the socialities, the press, and politics all receive satirical treatment. Other groups are caricatured as well: women over thirty, pompous provincials, and poseurs of every kind. Dickens' attitude is that of a humane skeptic. He sees through all types of deception and pretense, whether it is personal or institutional. Except when the deception is parasitic and corrupt, as it is in the law, Dickens enjoys pretense for its own sake, as part of the theater of life. Little people trying to puff themselves up is the eternal stuff of which comedy is made.

SENTIMENT

Sentiment is a way of viewing the world complementary to that of comedy. It is based on the recognition that certain situations are not reducible to comedy; the frustration and imprisonment of a good man, for example. It then tries to make literary capital of poignant situations. As comedy tries to draw laughter, sentiment tries to draw tears. In the eighteenth century these two modes were frequently mixed, and Dickens combined them in *Pickwick Papers*. Sentiment is not at all close to tragedy, however, since it depicts sad situations more or less for their own sake.

Comedy is by far the dominant mode of the novel, but sentiment crops up at frequent intervals. The interpolated tales tend to exploit the pathos of innocent victims of evil. In the tale about Prince Bladud, Dickens goes further and treats sentiment in a jocular way, but this is unsuccessful. In fact, Dickens generally fails when he tries to exploit sentiment in these tales, not merely because their style is so wretched, but because the situations themselves are obviously artificial.

However, Dickens is more successful with sentiment when he deals with Mr. Pickwick's stay in prison. Here the sentiment is integrated into its context; it fits the prison environment. The deathbed pathos of the Chancery prisoner is exactly what one might expect under the circumstances. Moreover, Dickens balances his bitter sadness with other points of view about prison, so it is not really obtrusive.

THE INTERPOLATED TALES

The interpolated tales are of little account from a literary standpoint. In general they are badly written and out of keeping with the comic tone of the novel. But they do bear a relation to the large themes of the novel, presenting those themes in an opposite manner from which they are presented in the narrative proper. The contrast between these tales and the action of the novel could scarcely be greater. The mood and action of the tales are savage, violent, and luridly melodramatic. The father-son theme is treated as a brutal, unrelenting kind of warfare. Liquor, which is beneficient in the novel, becomes the source of alcoholic terrors in "The Stroller's Tale." And in the story of Gabriel Grub we see Mr. Pickwick's story written in reverse. If the mode of the novel is comedy, the mode of these tales is nightmare. One senses that Dickens was trying to grapple with his themes in all of their possibilities. The only way he could deal with their nightmarish aspect was to bracket it in the form of "tales."

CONTRAST

Contrast is the most important literary device in the novel. It is more important than comedy, sentiment, and nightmare because it includes each of these modes. We have seen how Dickens plays each of these methods against the others in a complementary way.

Dickens defines his characters through dramatic contrasts, by having them collide. In the collisions they reveal their essence. Mr. Pickwick stands at the center of the novel in a moral sense: everyone else is measured against him. Through these multiple contrasts we get a fully developed portrait of Mr. Pickwick: his attitudes toward women, friends, scoundrels, defeated enemies, mercenary marriages, disinterested love, travel, liquor, good food, pretense.

The result of Dickens' thoroughgoing use of contrast was to develop a method for exploring his themes, a method he would use in novel after novel with increasing success. By using characters to reflect various facets of an idea, Dickens found he could develop his fictional ideas in depth. This method is analogical; it creates a fictional world that is coherent because it is based on some central idea or metaphor. Shakespeare and Tolstoy also used this method extensively.

Dickens took this basic relationship and developed it into a moral spectrum ranging from the near-perfect Pickwick to the bestial characters of the interpolated tales; from the good Sam Weller to the dissipated Bob Sawyer and Ben Allen. Mr. Pickwick and Sam Weller would lack definition if they had not been tested against these other types. No matter how outrageous Dickens may be in his caricatures, he has developed a very sound method for giving his novels reality, subtlety, and depth.

THE PICKWICK CLUB

The idea of the Pickwick Club is the nucleus from which the novel grows. Once the action is under way the club is more or less discarded. In Chapter 1 we see the club in session. In Chapter 11 we are reminded of its existence, and then we forget about it until the end of the book, when Mr. Pickwick announces in a line or two that the club is dissolved.

The club is originally presented as a society for the gathering and dissemination of "scientific" knowledge. Mr. Pickwick undertakes his travels to collect curiosities and examine local customs. The club is an object of satire, of course, and Mr. Pickwick is a rather pompous old gentleman. To continue the club idea would mean perpetuating Mr. Pickwick as a caricature. Dickens clearly had other ideas for his development.

Mr. Pickwick's companions, Tupman, Snodgrass, and Winkle, are club members, but we forget this. In other words, the idea of the club is transformed into the idea of a group of friends under Mr. Pickwick's patronage. Their object becomes travel for its own sake, for fun and romance, rather than for information. Thus Dickens turns a rather sterile conception into something flexible and rich with possibility.

Blotton, a club member who habitually tells the truth in a harsh way, is discarded in Chapter 11. But his function of telling the truth is taken over by the genial Sam Weller, who makes it possible for Mr. Pickwick to develop into a figure of high comedy rather than an object of farce.

In Chapter 39, with the episode of the scientific gentleman, Dickens measures the good Mr. Pickwick against his farcical beginnings in a rather pompous old man with pretentions to scientific knowledge. This device not only works, it is amusing.

STYLE

From the full title of the novel, *The Posthumous Papers of the Pickwick Club,* one might expect a collection of notes, letters, diaries, and minutes. Yet from the first the narrative takes a different form. The narrator, "Boz," is purportedly reworking the club papers into a coherent, unified story. However, before we are very far along the machinery of the club and the note-taking by the Pickwickians are forgotten. And what emerges is an omniscient third-person narrator.

This narrator has special predilections. While he can enter the minds of his characters and read their thoughts, this mode is not really congenial to him. He prefers to show off his characters as if they were on stage, to present them dramatically through their appearance, their gestures and, above all, their speech. The characters talk themselves alive, so to speak. Dickens is a protean author, able to project himself through hundreds of distinct, lively roles. His delight in play-acting is evident everywhere. Even in making fun of theatrical pretenses he enjoys their exuberance.

Dickens' sense of theater gives the action of *Pickwick Papers* a sense of immediacy. We can visualize the scenes taking place before our eyes. Although Dickens uses the past tense, we imagine the action happening in the present. It is not enough to say that Dickens has a quick, brilliant eye and a reportorial ear. He also has the intense imagination needed to make his invented characters come alive.

The portrait of Dickens that this novel conveys is one of a witty, shrewd, observant, flexible, inventive, humane young man. The prose itself is ironic, colloquial, supple, fresh, adaptable to many moods and situations. Most important, it is playful, open to experiment. We realize the youthfulness of the narrative voice, but we are also astonished frequently at its artistic maturity. It is by means of this voice that the reader participates in the ebullience of the novel. If this book celebrates freedom, plenty, innocence, openheartedness, and youth, it does so mainly through the spirited prose and mimicry.

SETTING

COACHING DAYS

Pickwick Papers is set in southern England in the years of 1827 to 1831. Among other things this novel gave an enduring literary expression to the "coaching days" period of English life. As Dickens was writing his novel that period was rapidly being destroyed by the new railroads. An air of nostalgia seems to hang about the coaches, coachmen, macadam roads, and wayside inns that fill the book. Dickens, in fact, played a large part in creating the romance of the coach through his treatment of it in this novel.

Coaches are an important part of the book. Several coach rides are described in detail, usually in a spirit of exhilaration, anticipation, and gaiety. Coaches transport the Pickwickians to almost every place they visit, forming a connecting link between the various adventures. However, coaches are also a source of adventure in themselves. Mr. Pickwick and his friends become acquainted with a number of fateful characters during coach rides, notably Jingle, Peter Magnus, and Captain Dowler. Further, one interpolated tale revolves around the adventure in a deserted mail coach. Coaches facilitate adventures because they throw strangers into one another's company for hours.

Coaches were a fast means of travel at that time, and one gets a sense of their speed along paved roads with relays of horses. Seldom does a journey take more than a day, and Mr. Pickwick can move across southern England, from London to Bath, in about a day. Dickens felt pride in the speed and regularity of coach trips, and he felt affection for colorful coachmen like Tony Weller.

A corollary to this world of travel is the inn or hotel where travelers stop to dine and sleep. There are more than two dozen such places mentioned in the novel, with names like "The White Hart Inn," "The Marquis of Granby," and "The Leathern Bottle." Quaint English inns abound in Mr. Pickwick's travels. Yet for all their quaintness they were attuned to the efficiency of coach travel, kept relays of horses for stopping coaches, and were clean and comfortable. Dickens delights in describing these inns, knowing them very well from his days as a traveling reporter. After hours in a coach they must have seemed especially cosy and inviting.

LOCALE

Dickens does something very interesting with the various locales the Pickwickians visit. Each is given a distinct emotional coloring according to the action that takes place there, but the action is a reflection of Mr. Pickwick's education. By this we mean that what happens to Mr. Pickwick in the places he visits has a direct bearing on his stage of development, and vice versa. There is a definite pattern to the locales.

At the hub of the novel is London, the home base of the Pick-wickians. This is the center to which Mr. Pickwick makes periodic returns. London is also the place where most of Mr. Pickwick's education takes place, the moral testing ground, as it were.

When Mr. Pickwick and his friends head for Rochester they are as innocent and gullible as very young boys. The Rochester area, which includes Dingley Dell, lies due east of London. And through the adventures that happen there we come to associate the area with knock-about farce and trusting innocence. Dingley Dell represents a kind of Eden.

When Mr. Pickwick and Mr. Wardle chase Jingle to London, London acquires associations of dishonesty and sharpness. Mr. Pickwick returns to Dingley Dell only to leave it immediately. His innocence has been badly dented, and he returns to London.

The next series of adventures takes place in an area northeast of London, at Eatanswill (Norwich), Bury St. Edmunds, and Ipswich. The keynote to this area is deception. There is the wirepulling behind the Eatanswill election, the fakery of the Hunter party, the practical joke of Jingle and Job Trotter at Bury St. Edmunds, and the delusions of the Nupkins at Ipswich. In the middle of this section Mr. Pickwick makes a short visit to London because he is enmeshed in a concocted lawsuit, and London acquires further associations of chicanery.

After all of this emphasis on deception Mr. Pickwick and his friends make a Christmas trip to Dingley Dell, as if to recharge Mr. Pickwick's faith in human goodness.

Back in London legal trickery wins as Mr. Pickwick loses the lawsuit. The Pickwickians then go to Bath, which lies west of London. Bath is a center of social snobbery, but Mr. Pickwick goes to Bristol, where he finds himself involved in aiding Winkle's romance. At this point the emphasis of the novel begins to change. Deception fades as Mr. Pickwick's positive qualities come to the fore.

In London again, Mr. Pickwick goes to debtors' prison for three months. London begins to seem like the meanest, most treacherous, saddest place on earth from the inside of prison. But Mr. Pickwick changes this as he displays forgiveness and charity toward his enemies and self-sacrifice toward Sam Weller. Mr. Pickwick and Sam rise above the squalor of prison; they single-handedly humanize the place for us. Once they are released London loses much of its nastiness.

Mr. Pickwick then undertakes a romantic adventure to Bristol and Birmingham on behalf of the Winkles, and these locales take on some of this excitement. Finally, back in London romance takes charge as the courtships and marriages have happy conclusions.

Thus London changes as Mr. Pickwick does, and the various locales take their emotional coloring from his spiritual state. His progress changes the focus of events, which in turn gives each geographical area its special flavor. While we view Mr. Pickwick largely from the outside, Dickens conveys his growth by means of the action, by the way he focuses on the adventures. In this way Dickens was able to show us his hero's internal development through external events. The method is really quite subtle.

ITINERARY AND TIME SCHEME

PERSONS	TRIP	TIME	CHAPTER
Pickwickians	London to Rochester	May 13, 1827	2
Pickwickians	Rochester to Dingley Dell	May, 1827	5
Pickwick and Wardle	Dingley Dell to London	May, 1827	9
Pickwick and Wardle	London to Dingley Dell	June, 1827	10
Pickwickians	Dingley Dell to Cobham	June, 1827	11
Pickwickians	Cobham to London	June, 1827	11
Pickwickians	London to Eatanswill	Aug., 1830	13
Pickwick	Eatanswill to Bury St. Edmunds	Aug., 1830	16
Pickwick	Bury St. Edmunds to London	Sept., 1830	20
Pickwick	London to Ipswich	Sept., 1830	22
Pickwickians	Ipswich to London	Dec. ?, 1830	25
Sam Weller	London to Dorking and back	Dec. ?, 1830	27
Pickwickians	London to Dingley Dell	Dec., 1830	28
Pickwickians	Dingley Dell to London	Jan., 1831	30
Pickwickians	London to Bath	Feb., 1831	35

Persons	Trip	Time	Chapter
Winkle and Pickwick	Bath to Bristol and back	April ?, 1831	38 & 39
Pickwickians	Bath to London	April, 1831	39
Pickwick	London to Bristol	July, 1831	48
Pickwick	Bristol to Birmingham	July, 1831	50
Pickwick	Birmingham to London	July, 1831	51
Sam Weller	London to Dorking	Aug., 1831	52
Sam Weller	Dorking to London	Aug., 1831	55
Pickwick	London to Dulwich	Aug., 1831	57

The first thing one might notice about this time scheme is its irregularity. For one thing the action begins in 1827 and suddenly jumps to 1830. In the course of writing the novel, which was published serially, Dickens forgot his original date. Despite this mix-up the action of the novel takes about a year and four months.

The reader gets a clear idea of how long each adventure takes because Dickens usually gives a day-to-day account of it from beginning to end. In a sense, each adventure is a time capsule of successive days. However, the dates are out of keeping with our day-to-day sense of time. Mr. Pickwick presumably goes to Ipswich in September, stays no more than a week, and gets back to London in December! Time is speeded up to give a sense of consecutive adventures, one following hard upon another, even when this contradicts our sense of time's daily passage in the novel. The time logic is therefore closer to that of dreams than to waking reality. What makes this use of time unobtrusive is the extraordinary richness of invention that Dickens gives to the adventures. No author could get away with this in a dull book.

Something else one might notice is the great number of places visited. Imaginary spots like Dingley Dell mingle with real towns like Rochester. And one imaginary name, Eatanswill, is a disguise for Norwich, used because of the satirical treatment of the place.

In general the adventures tend to be grouped in various locales, with London as the center. The early adventures are set in the Rochester area, east of London. The next series take place in a locale northeast of London. The final set of adventures lie to the west of London, at Bath, Bristol, and Birmingham. So the settings tend to move counterclockwise around London.

Both time and geography are used subjectively. Time is employed to give the adventures a comic, hurried rhythm. And geography acquires an emotional coloring that conveys Mr. Pickwick's moral development.

REVIEW QUESTIONS

1. Show the stages of Mr. Pickwick's moral development.

2. What part does Jingle play in Mr. Pickwick's development? Mrs. Bardell? Dodson and Fogg? Fleet Prison? Nathaniel Winkle?

3. What part does Sam Weller play in Mr. Pickwick's growth as a character? Describe the stages of their relationship.

4. How does Dickens use various locales to define Mr. Pickwick's growth?

5. Trace Alfred Jingle's career. How does it parallel Mr. Pickwick's?

6. Do you feel that Dickens was justified in changing Jingle's character in the Fleet? Give your reasons.

7. Delineate various father-son relationships in the novel and show how they reflect on each other.

8. How does Dickens treat young women in this book? Middle-aged women?

9. Is Dickens successful in handling friendship? Romance? Explain his relative success or failure.

10. Show some of the major ways in which Dickens uses contrast.

11. How do the interpolated tales reflect the action of the novel? Take one of the tales and illustrate this.

12. Describe Dickens' prose style.

13. Take an episode, such as Mr. Pickwick's "proposal" to Mrs. Bardell (Chapter 12), and show some of its comic devices.

14. What is Dickens' attitude toward the legal profession?

15. What does Dingley Dell represent? How is it related to the rest of the novel?

16. Show the devices by which Dickens changes the mood of the novel during the Fleet Prison sequence.

17. How does Dickens restore the comic tone once the prison episode is finished?

18. What part does Bob Sawyer play in restoring the comic mood?

19. Discuss the loose time scheme of the novel. Why does Dickens speed up time?

20. Compare Mr. Pickwick to a picaresque hero like Tom Jones or Don Quixote.

21. Do you think this novel deserves the epithet "great"? Give your reasons, taking care to define the criteria of "greatness" in literature.

SELECTED BIBLIOGRAPHY

CHESTERTON, G. K. *Charles Dickens.* New York: Schocken Books, 1965. An enthusiastic, delightful appreciation of Dickens, with excellent comments on *Pickwick Papers.*

COCKSHUT, A. O. J. *The Imagination of Charles Dickens.* London: Butler & Tanner, Ltd., 1961. A thoughtful, well-written essay on the major themes and novels of Dickens.

DABNEY, ROSS H. *Love and Property in the Novels of Dickens.* London: Chatto & Windus, 1967. Absorbing study of two related themes in all the major novels.

DYSON, A. E. *Dickens: Modern Judgements.* London: Macmillan & Co., 1968. Contains essays on each novel and varies in quality.

FIELDING, K. J. *Charles Dickens: A Critical Introduction*. New York: Longmans, Green & Co., 1958. A sound basic survey of Dickens' life and novels.

FORD, GEORGE H. *Dickens and His Readers*. Princeton, N.J.: Princeton University Press, 1955. An intelligent account of the intimate relationship Dickens had with his readers, and a survey of Dickens' critical reputation.

FORSTER, JOHN. *The Life of Charles Dickens*. New York: Doubleday, Doran & Co., 1928. Still an indispensable source on Dickens by a close friend.

GISSING, GEORGE. *Critical Studies of the Works of Charles Dickens*. London: Blackie & Son, Ltd., 1898. Excellent early study of Dickens' novels.

HOUSE, HUMPHRY. *The Dickens World*. New York: Oxford University Press, 1941. A good study of the relationship between Dickens' novels, his thought, and the Victorian context.

JOHNSON, EDGAR. *Charles Dickens: His Triumph and Tragedy*. New York: Simon & Shuster, Inc., 1952. The definitive biography, containing chapters on the novels.

MARCUS, STEVEN. *Dickens: From Pickwick to Dombey*. New York: Basic Books, Inc., 1965. A fine, penetrating critical work on Dickens' first seven novels.

MILLER, J. HILLIS. *Charles Dickens: The World of His Novels*. Cambridge, Mass.: Harvard University Press, 1958. A close, often penetrating look at Dickens' symbolic and thematic elements, but flimsy on *Pickwick Papers*.

WILSON, EDMUND. *The Wound and the Bow: Seven Studies in Literature*. Boston: Houghton Mifflin Co., 1941. A stimulating attempt to relate Dickens' psychology to his fiction.

YOUNG, G. M. *Victorian England: Portrait of an Age*. New York: Oxford University Press, 1953. The best introduction to the Victorian period ever written; an outstanding work.

NOTES

NOTES

NOTES

NOTES

NOTES

NOTES

NOTES